thing only: the world would be a different place."

During the passage of time, Rovere notes, Communism was raised from an ideology to a theology and McCarthyism flourished and fell; John Foster Dulles traveled the world giving away international "insurance policies" which we are still bound to honor; China has now become more menacing than Russia. At home, a new awareness of poverty and racism has arisen and the first groping efforts to correct their evils have been made; and we are beginning to become conscious of the enormous waste of our natural resources.

General Marshall's twenty years have passed. Have the American people changed their attitude? Will they ever be willing to undertake a limited war again? And what would be the effect of neo-isolationism on the United States internally, to say nothing of the United States' position in the world? These are the questions that Richard H. Rovere grapples with in one of the most agonizing documents to appear in recent years.

# Waist Deep
# in the Big Muddy

# Waist Deep
# in the Big Muddy

*Personal Reflections on 1968*

by

RICHARD H. ROVERE

*An Atlantic Monthly Press Book*

LITTLE, BROWN AND COMPANY · BOSTON · TORONTO

LIBRARY OF CONGRESS CATALOG CARD NO. 68–22900

FIRST EDITION

The title of this book was suggested by the song "Waist Deep in the Big Muddy," words and music by Pete Seeger. Copyright © 1967 by TRO-Melody Trails, Inc., New York.

A considerable portion of this book appeared originally in *The New Yorker*, in somewhat different form.

ATLANTIC–LITTLE, BROWN BOOKS
ARE PUBLISHED BY
LITTLE, BROWN AND COMPANY
IN ASSOCIATION WITH
THE ATLANTIC MONTHLY PRESS

*Published simultaneously in Canada
by Little, Brown & Company (Canada) Limited*

PRINTED IN THE UNITED STATES OF AMERICA

*For*
*William Shawn*

# Contents

# Waist Deep
# in the Big Muddy

# I

# Presidents and Their Wars

This is not 1948; LBJ is not Harry Truman; and
Vietnam is not Korea.
—From an editorial in the *New
Republic*, September 30, 1967

Some of us who were well beyond the age of consent in 1948 and 1950 must now square past and
present. The young need not trouble their minds or
their consciences about what went on in the Dark
Ages, but those over thirty-five or forty must in one
way or another confront certain moral, political, and
intellectual problems created for them by the views
they held two decades ago. Consistency may be a
mean virtue, but many people prize it highly and go
to remarkable lengths to show others and themselves
that they possess it.

It is always easier to deny than to establish the
validity of any given historical analogy. If history
really repeated itself, its study would be at once bor-
ing and terrifying. But analogy can have a limited

validity and can, like metaphor, yield and enrich insights. Moreover, where a denial is so flat and emphatic, it is advisable to take a close, hard look. Why should anyone insist that "this is not 1948"? We can keep track of the years without assistance. Why bring up 1948 instead of 1964 or 1952—or, for that matter, 1776? Why not say that Lyndon Johnson isn't Calvin Coolidge or the Shah of Iran, and that the war in Vietnam isn't the Mexican War or the Wars of the Roses? Clearly, the years, men, and events juxtaposed by the *New Republic* have, or appear to have, something in common.

There is, as it happens, one quite striking resemblance between the Presidential politics of 1968 and the Presidential politics of 1948. Then, as now, many liberal Democrats wished very much to be rid of a liberal Democratic President. Though in the end most of them probably voted for Harry Truman against Thomas E. Dewey, a few supported that year's "peace" candidate—Henry A. Wallace, who had recently resigned the editorship of the *New Republic*—and others, early in the year, had made strenuous efforts to get the Democratic Party to dump Truman and name as its candidate the then Chief of Staff of the United States Army, Dwight D. Eisenhower. (Improbable as it sounds, General Eisenhower might be described as the Robert Kennedy of 1948. Eisenhower declined to become involved, although it is said that when he was approached on this matter by some leaders of Americans for Democratic Action, his response was that he would consider accepting the Democratic nomination if he could get the Republican one as well.) True, the motives of the 1948 liberals were quite different from those that spur today's liberals into disowning Johnson and contemplating support for a conservative Republican, provided he is less of a hawk than the President. The dump-Truman people* did not hate the then President; they merely scorned him and feared that the Democratic Party could not win with him. What the dump-Johnson people fear is precisely the opposite—a Democratic victory that would keep the despised incumbent in office. The dump-Truman people, like everyone else, believed the opinion polls, and they didn't want to be stuck with a loser; the dump-Johnson liberals, also with an eye on the polls, don't want to be stuck with a winner.

---

* According to Cabell Phillips in the *New York Times* for October 22, 1967, Truman was himself at one point a dump-Truman liberal. With the certitude of one who got it from the horse's mouth—or from two horses' mouths—Phillips asserts that in November 1947, Truman called Eisenhower to the White House and offered the General the Democratic nomination for President and the services of Harry Truman as a candidate for Vice-President.

"LBJ is not Harry Truman." In many ways, they are as different as John F. Kennedy and William Howard Taft. Johnson is a consummate politician; Truman was only a persevering one. Truman was as artless as Johnson is artful. Truman was generally candid, and Johnson seems a compulsive dissembler. One could go on. Truman's foreign policy was widely admired and more often than not was successful, but in domestic policy he never got anywhere; Johnson has done quite well with domestic policy, but his foreign policy may lead us all to disaster. Still, Johnson in 1968 has more in common with Truman in 1948 than the hostility of some of the same liberals. Both were once Democratic senators and Vice-Presidents. Each took office upon the death of a beloved predecessor. Johnson, like Truman, has never been a child of the Establishment. From the Eastern liberals' point of view, both came from the wrong, or South, side of the tracks. Both had meager, or at least unfashionable, schooling. Both have rather coarse manners and offend by indelicacy of speech. (Liberals, I have no doubt, consider themselves large-minded people, concerned with principles, not personalities. Some are large-minded, others not. If Kennedy had lived, he might at some point have called a halt to the escalation he began. He might even have found a way to get us out of Vietnam altogether. If he had lived and, as seems to me entirely possible, found no better solution than Johnson's, then, of course, he would have faced today much the kind of opposition that Johnson faces. But I cannot help believing that it would have been somewhat less widespread and more restrained against a Commander-in-Chief who was a Harvard man with uncommon wit, intellectual poise, a passion for excellence, and gallantry of manner. Kennedy just might have managed to run a slightly more stylish war.) But the relevant thing is that Johnson is, as Truman was, a liberal Democratic President of the United States in serious trouble on almost every front. Though Truman failed where Johnson has more or less succeeded, and vice versa, their policies are very similar, causing them to make the same enemies.

Truman astonished everyone—including, I have always believed, himself—by winning in 1948, and the liberals, some of whom now seem to have forgotten that they ever opposed him, were gratified at being spared a Republican administration. A year and a half later, we were at war in Korea. There was some opposition to our intervention, but most of it came from isolationists, like Joseph P. Kennedy and Herbert Hoover. Little of it came from the liberals. Wayne Morse, J. William Fulbright, Arthur Schlesinger, Jr., and J. Kenneth Galbraith all had the public ear in those days, but although Senator (then Representative) Fulbright had called for Truman's resignation as early as 1946, none of these estimable men was critical of our involvement in Korea—and neither, it may be well to say, was I, who now share with them a thoroughgoing disapproval of our policy in Vietnam. They were in varying degrees enthusiastic in their support of that intervention, even when General Douglas MacArthur, with the full backing of his American superiors and with a special mandate from the United Nations General Assembly, escalated the war by invading North Korea —a step that is held by most historians to have brought the Chinese into the war.* There was, to be sure, severe criticism, largely led by liberals fearing a full-scale war with China, of MacArthur's subse-

---

* It was not quite so clear at the time as most people think it is today that the Chinese intervened because MacArthur had crossed the thirty-eighth parallel. Some attached more importance to the President's decision to put the Seventh Fleet in the Strait of Taiwan than to his simultaneous orders to assist the Republic of Korea. On August 25, 1950, when American troops still had their backs to the sea on the Pusan beachhead in South Korea, Chou En-lai, the foreign minister, told the United Nations that "the people of China . . . are determined to liberate from the tentacles of the United States aggressors Taiwan and all other territories belonging to China." Throughout those months, Chinese propaganda laid far more stress on what it called our "open encroachment on the territory of the People's Republic of China" than on our conflict with North Korea.

quent politicking for further escalation, but that came after, not before, administration policy had led to a greatly widened war in Korea. MacArthur's original move north—surely analogous to an invasion of North Vietnam today—was regarded as an altogether legitimate pursuit of altogether legitimate aims.

Though I supported the war in Korea, I oppose the war in Vietnam—not because I think it odious by comparison with any earlier war or intervention but for a variety of other reasons, mostly having to do with the passage of time and with changes that have taken place throughout the world and in the United States. Because I regard its termination as the most urgent task this country now faces, I may in 1968 vote for Lyndon Johnson's opponent. If I do so, it will not be because I agree with Dr. Benjamin Spock, who also supported the war in Korea and who in October 1967 told the peace marchers on the Mall in Washington that "Lyndon Johnson is the enemy," but rather because I agree with General George Catlett Marshall that it is a melancholy truth of politics and statesmanship that "to change a policy, you must change the men." I have written much in dispraise of Johnson, but I do not think him a wicked man, and I believe that he was a splendid President in the first years after John Kennedy's death and might be a great one today if it were not for this war. I am aware of no evidence that his conduct of it has been less circumspect than Truman's conduct of the earlier war or that he has betrayed any trust or promise that any of his recent predecessors honored.

"Vietnam is not Korea." They are two thousand miles apart and markedly different in climate, terrain, and demography. The two Vietnams are larger than the two Koreas by forty-two thousand square miles. Koreans outnumber Vietnamese by six million. Both, however, are relatively small and underdeveloped Asian countries partitioned into a Communist North and a non-Communist South by international agreements in the making of which they had no voice. Both abut China, both are peninsular, and both have long histories of colonial occupation and oppression. Each in the mid-twentieth century has been the site of large-scale warfare, with the United States in each case intervening to assist the anti-Communist government of the Southern region, and with China and the Soviet Union assisting—on a considerable scale in Korea and on what is still a limited scale in Vietnam—the Communist regime in the North.

There are other parallels and, of course, many

divergencies. History does not repeat itself. Vietnam's relationship to Soviet and Chinese power in 1968 is very different from—and vastly more complicated than—that of Korea in 1950. Though before 1950 there had been general agreement that Korea was outside our "defense perimeter," its proximity to Japan gave it a strategic importance that cannot be claimed for Vietnam. In Korea, the action was purely military. There was no "other war" to be fought there—no "pacification" behind the front, no "revolutionary development" to be carried on to secure peasant loyalties. The political situation in Korea may have been far from ideal and anything but "democratic"; it was, though, relatively stable. In South Vietnam, religious and political differences plague the life of the country and constantly threaten what passes for national unity in what is not yet a nation. If there were any such threats to Korean unity, Syngman Rhee's iron hand kept them in check. Now and then, it is true, some disaffected students made public displays of their dislike for the regime and were disciplined in rather primitive ways. But in the main the regime we supported in Korea could pretty well hold its own, while the one we support in Vietnam thinks it is doing well when it can claim control of half of the territory it maintains it has the right to govern. Charleton Ogburn,

Jr., a former State Department Asian expert, has argued with some force that the Korea-Vietnam analogy breaks down altogether when one analyzes the status of the belligerents vis-à-vis the great powers. North Korea, he says, was a puppet through and through, while the Republic of Korea—South Korea—was an "indigenous political expression" of Korean nationalism. In Vietnam, on the contrary, it is the Northern Communist regime that is genuinely nationalist, while our friends in the South— led so largely by generals from the North who once served with the French—are spurious in their nationalism and manifestly play the role of an American puppet.

From some perspectives, the divergencies may be more important than the parallels. But as I see it, only one of them, the different relationships of North Vietnam and North Korea to the Soviet Union and China, bears centrally on the soundness of our present policy. In any consideration of this matter, we must, I think, begin with the incontrovertible fact that the two countries are on the same continent. In both cases, United States policy in Asia has been at issue. This has been the key to the thinking of one American liberal, Walter Lippmann, who would have no difficulty in finding in the public record proof positive of his own consistency. Long

before we became involved in the Korean war, Lippmann was saying that this country had no business
whatever deploying its troops on the mainland of
Asia. At the time of Korea, he said that we should be
involved, if at all, only as a sea and air power, and he
has been saying the same thing about Vietnam for
several years. In this, he is only invoking an established (though perhaps today disestablished) American doctrine, and, as a matter of fact, that doctrine
was briefly in force even after President Truman and
his advisers had committed us to the defense of
South Korea on June 25, 1950.*

In Vietnam we have again tested the wisdom of
the doctrine abandoned eighteen years ago, and to
many of us its essential soundness has again been
demonstrated. But a much larger question is
whether we have any business entering any Asian
wars with any kind of American power. It is difficult
to see how anyone could maintain that it was mor-

---

* Though it tends to be forgotten now, those who—in
Blair House, on that important date—agreed that we ought
to intervene had in mind giving the South Koreans only
such support as our Navy and Air Force could supply. And
for three days that was all we gave. It was not until President Truman was personally assured that General Mac-
Arthur, who had been up to then a leading member of the
Lippmann school (MacArthur had once said that anyone
who advocated the use of our ground forces in Asia "ought
to have his head examined"), had changed his mind that
the President assented to the historic shift in policy.

ally right to enter an Asian dispute in 1950 and is morally wrong to do the same thing today. A more valid argument can be offered on the ground that what makes the one intervention defensible and the other indefensible is that in the interval between the two wars what we once called "international Communism" has been shown to be nonexistent. What in 1950 appeared to be "monolithic" is now revealed as "polycentric." This is an enormously important and highly relevant development, but it does not really alter the basic question of what our role in Asia should be. Even if no Communist powers had been involved in either case, or if the ally of one Northern regime had been Communist and the ally of the other had been anti-Communist, it would still be necessary to decide how much responsibility this country should assume for a balance of power in Asia.

Do we, as a people, have any morally or politically legitimate concern with the political order in Asia? If we say no—or say perhaps, but not to the point of using force—then we simply have to ask ourselves what on earth we were doing in Korea eighteen years ago, and even what we were fighting the Japanese about twenty-five years ago. (It will not do to say that they attacked us at Pearl Harbor. That would not have happened if our foreign policy had not threatened theirs.) For, beyond all the talk about Fascism and imperialism and Communism and democracy and self-determination, the basic reality is that, for bad reasons or good, the United States has with increasing frequency throughout most of this century been throwing its weight around in Asia to create or maintain a political order that several American governments have decided is best for the United States and possibly best for Asia. It can be argued that we would all be far better off if this decision had never been taken by anyone, but it was taken—and not by Lyndon Johnson in late 1963 or early 1964.* The balance of power—that is what our three Asian wars have been about, and we might as well state the rest of this proposition, which is that this is what all foreign policy is and almost always has been about. If we ask ourselves why we shouldn't leave the balance of power in Asia to the Asians, we might as well reopen the question of whether we have, or ever had, any business messing about with the balance of power in Europe or anywhere else in the world or the cosmos. I can think of

---

* If a date has to be fixed, it might be well to settle on February 6, 1899, when the Senate ratified—with one vote more than the required two-thirds—the Treaty of Paris, which ended the war with Spain and provided for the annexation of the Philippines. This led Theodore Roosevelt to get on with the digging of the Panama Canal and the building of a two-ocean Navy.

several quite compelling arguments for having different European and Asian policies, but I cannot see how the war in Vietnam can be regarded as some new and lamentable departure from established policy. Rather, it appears to me an application of established policy that has miscarried so dreadfully that we must begin examining not just the case at hand but the whole works. If this is where our foreign policy lands us, then we had better settle among ourselves whether the policy is, or ever was, any good.

For many, the real clincher is that, as they see it now, in Korea we opposed an act of clear and premeditated aggression carried out by an army crossing an international boundary and seeking to annex by force the territory on the other side, whereas in Vietnam we are interfering in what is essentially a civil war, with the forces we oppose consisting mostly of indigenous rebels. There is something in this, but, in my view, very little, and nothing, certainly, to destroy the strength of the analogy. Koreans fought Koreans in Korea, as Vietnamese are fighting Vietnamese in Vietnam. In each case, the issue was control of the Southern territory and unification of the country. In each case, the contested area has been part of the homeland of people with a more or less common history. Indeed, it can, it seems, be argued that the partition of Vietnam into Northern and Southern regions has greater historical justification than the similar partition of Korea. Many historians maintain that the cultural and political differences between North and South in Vietnam are large and ancient ones, difficult to resolve under one government. "By 1620," according to John T. McAlister, Jr., a Princeton authority on Southeast Asia, writing in *World Politics* for January 1967, "the system had succumbed to regional pressures, and Vietnam had become divided into two warring states, literally separated by a wall built across the width of the country at the eighteenth parallel near the town of Dong Hoi, north of Hué." This seventeenth-century anti-infiltration barrier, McAlister goes on, was "constructed by the leaders of the southern faction, the Nguyen family, [and] rose to a height of eighteen feet. . . . [In] 1672 it proved strong enough to withstand a major military test by the northern faction under the generalship of the Trinh family." Korea had known partitions since 108 B.C. Nevertheless, Edwin O. Reischauer writes that it "is a more homogeneous national unit than are most of the countries of South Asia." As for the "boundary" at the Thirty-eighth Parallel in Korea, though it had been proposed as a line of demarcation between Russian and Japanese spheres of influence following the war in 1905, the State Department used to describe it as a "fortuitous line resulting from the exigencies of war." Secretary of State James Byrnes had in 1947 called it "a military convenience."

In any event, Americans should be the last people to say that a civil war is not a civil war when it is primarily regional in character, when it can more or less accurately be described as a War Between the States, and when it is fought by massed armies.

In his *Memoirs 1925–1950*, George F. Kennan, who was director of the State Department's Policy Planning Staff until late in 1949, writes of Korea: "This was, finally, a civil conflict, not an international one; and the term 'aggression' in the usual international sense was as misplaced here as it was to be later in the case of Vietnam." Kennan nevertheless approved our intervention—indeed, thought it an inescapable duty. Until 1945, Korea had been a Japanese colony. We accepted the Japanese surrender in the Southern zone. But in 1950, he says, "There was as yet no peace treaty with Japan to define [Korea's] future status. We had accepted the responsibilities of military occupation in South Korea, and the fact that we had withdrawn our own combat forces did not mean, in the continued absence of a Japanese peace treaty, that these responsibilities were terminated. We had a perfect right to intervene, on the basis of our position as occupying power, to assure the preservation of order in this territory."

Here is a distinction between the two wars that is also an important difference. Kennan—who, incidentally, opposed the bombing of North Korea, as today he opposes the bombing of North Vietnam—felt that we should have gone ahead in Korea without bringing in the United Nations, whose involvement, as he saw it, itself became a cause of heightened tensions. Most of today's older doves, however, maintain that the backing of the U.N. gave the earlier war a legitimacy that the present one lacks. Few things about the situation in which we now find ourselves should give us more concern than the fact that today we clearly do not enjoy the good opinion of much of mankind. But if the truth is to be told, we didn't enjoy it in the early fifties, either. The U.N. support was largely illusory and came about through dumb luck. The Russians had absentmindedly—and providentially, from our point of view—boycotted the U.N. Security Council, and were thus unable to veto the resolution of support. Had there been a Russian veto, the United States would have gone ahead without U.N. support. We were already in the war. Furthermore, the Security Council resolution was something less than an unequivocal call to arms. It called for a cease-fire and asked U.N. members to "render every assistance" in bringing one to pass. In a book on the war published in 1951,* Arthur Schlesinger, Jr., and I wrote: "By putting the broadest possible construction on this, the President was able to say that his decision was in furtherance of United Nations policy. This claim gave rise to a wrangle that still goes on in law schools."

Though Dean Rusk is no doubt statistically correct in saying that "the proportion of non-United States forces in South Vietnam is greater than [that of] non-United States forces in Korea," we did have a good deal more approval in 1950 than we have in 1967. But most of it came in the form of talk. Even those nations, like England, that gave us some military assistance were scared stiff that we might lead them into a world war, and kept beseeching us to get out of Korea on the best terms we could—which, in time, was what we did. The Communist nations and the radical parties everywhere accused us, as they do today, of conducting an imperialist crusade. If the war in Vietnam is in some sense "imperialist," as so many Americans have come to believe, so was the war in Korea.

---

* Originally issued as *The General and the President* and reissued in 1965 as *The MacArthur Controversy and American Foreign Policy.*

In any event, the ultimate soundness of a policy is not to be determined by who supports it and who does not. This is particularly the case when, as in the U.N., the count is of nation states. The fact that a majority of General Assembly members has regularly opposed the admission of mainland China does not lend any moral or political force to the wisdom of mainland China's exclusion. The fact that the Organization of American States voted overwhelming support, *ex post facto,* of the American intervention in the Dominican Republic in 1965 has never been regarded as an acceptable sanction for the dispatch of troops. There is no moral safety in numbers.

In Korea, as in Vietnam, our intervention was undertaken on Presidential initiative. War was never declared by Congress. Truman lacked even so questionable a mandate as the one that Congress gave Johnson in the 1964 Gulf of Tonkin resolution. Dean Rusk can lecture congressmen today about our obligations to the Southeast Asia Treaty Organization, but SEATO had not even been thought of in Dean Acheson's day. Yet I picked up an antiwar manifesto signed by many people who to my certain knowledge favored the Korean intervention and find them saying that because "Congress has not declared a war, as required by the Constitution," the war in Vietnam is "unconstitutional and illegal." For my part, I would be pleased if the Supreme Court ruled the war unconstitutional next Monday morning. But I cannot imagine a theory of the war or of the Constitution that would hold our presence in Vietnam to be in violation of our fundamental law and would not require the same judgment on our earlier presence in Korea, as well as on a good many earlier interventions.

Nor can I see that it would make much difference, morally or in any other way, if Congress did declare the existence of a state of war or if the Supreme Court certified the carnage as constitutional.* Can any legislature turn an unjust cause into a just one by an observance of due process? Slavery was "constitutional" until it was smashed in a war of dubious constitutionality. The signers of this antiwar manifesto were brought together by, they say, a common

---

* It may some day do exactly that—or exactly the opposite. On November 6, 1967, the Court declined to review the cases of three privates who had refused to serve in Vietnam on the ground that the war there was illegal. However, two justices, Potter Stewart and William O. Douglas, dissented and said that the soldiers' cases posed "questions of great magnitude." Mr. Justice Stewart said he thought it possible that the Gulf of Tonkin resolution was a "constitutionally . . . impermissible delegation of all or part of Congress's power to declare war." While it seems to me clear that war is by its nature extralegal and extraconstitutional—a "legal" war being a moral fiction—I would not deny that there is an immensely important and long unresolved question over the division of powers in foreign policy, which of course includes war-making. Jefferson recognized this and thought the framers of the Constitution had settled the

desire to assist young men in avoiding conscription. A worthy purpose it may well be, but the draft is legal; the Selective Service Act has been in force for twenty-eight years, and the Supreme Court has yet to strike it down. I find the names of some of them also attached to an appeal calling upon other citizens to join them and Henry David Thoreau—part of whose "Civil Disobedience" is used as the manifesto for this particular group—in withholding from the Internal Revenue Service that part of their taxes which, by their calculations, "is being used to finance the war." The income tax laws are at least as legal and constitutional as Selective Service. Thoreau didn't want to help pay for the Mexican War, which may have been, as he passionately believed it was, immoral, but it was certainly not illegal or unconstitutional.

---

matter smartly. "We have already given in example," he wrote Madison in 1789, "one effectual check to the Dog of war by transferring the power of letting him loose from the Executive to the Legislative body, from those who are to spend to those who are to pay." It wasn't as effectual a check as he thought. Before long he was himself, as President, ordering the Navy to open fire on the Barbary Coast pirates, and later applauding the Monroe Doctrine, under the cover of which many Presidents have acted belligerently without congressional approval. The question may be one of life-and-death importance, but whatever action any court may take, I think it fundamentally unsusceptible of any "legal" solution.

# II

# The People
# We Have Become

When passions are engaged, the rhetoric of politics is almost always opportunistic—beware of mine!
—and that of the liberal doves is no more so than that of the liberal hawks or anyone else. If I have dealt at some length with liberal rhetoric, it is because it has become the lingua franca of that part of the Vietnam debate that is something more than a shouting match. The dispute has turned largely on whether the Johnson administration has carried on or betrayed policies that have in the main been set by liberal (and Democratic) Presidents from Woodrow Wilson to John F. Kennedy—and have on occasion, as in the Eisenhower years, been ratified and implemented by conservatives. Thus, the President insists that in Vietnam we are steadfastly up-

holding the right to "self-determination," while his critics, who honor the same tradition, argue that in Vietnam American arms are being used to deny that right. The President holds that his strategy is that of "containment," applied successfully and with almost universal approval in Europe twenty years ago, and his opponents say that containment, an admirable policy when applied in the right places by the right means against the right adversary, was never intended for use in South Vietnam. These are not irrelevant or uninteresting questions, but it seems to me that an excessive or exclusive concern with them enables debaters of both sides to take false comfort from false history. They deflect us from the urgent and difficult task of getting a true fix on where we are in 1968—on what kind of world we now inhabit and what kind of people we have become.

With the passage of time, Pascal wrote, "we all change and are no longer the same persons. Neither the offender nor the offended is the same." This view of time and life, as I shall later contend, was fundamental in the thinking of those who, twenty years ago, set American diplomacy on the course it has adhered to ever since and is presently adhering to, with increasingly disastrous results, in Vietnam. It has not, however, been fundamental in the thinking of those—most of them men of a liberal persuasion, as Daniel Patrick Moynihan has frequently reminded us—who have been executing the policy of late. To be sure, there have been acknowledgments of certain changes in the ways of the offender—the Soviet Union and some other Communist states—and some adaptations in strategy. But it has not, to the best of my knowledge, been suggested by any responsible figure that the passage of time may have invalidated either the entire policy or major parts of it. Nor has it been suggested that we—in our own view, the offended—have changed in ways that may make the policy no longer a fitting expression of our national character, no longer an instrumentality suitable to our purposes in the world.

Twenty years ago, we had, as a people, the self-righteous zeal of crusaders and the kind of energy crusaders need. Though self-righteousness is never attractive, ours was of a sort in many ways less repellent than most. We had played what we and most of the world's peoples regarded as an honorable and characteristically efficient part in destroying a system of tyranny as hateful as any the modern world had known. We had fought not as narrow nationalists but as internationalists, not as colonialists but as anticolonialists who, at the war's end, were as eager to see the empires of our allies liquidated as we had been to break up those of our enemies. We had great hopes for the United Nations—foolish hopes, as some felt at the time, yet anything but ignoble ones —and we were determined that it would not fail for any lack of confidence or effort on our part. There was then little dissent—and, compared with today, little cause for dissent—from the proposition that militant, militarized Communism threatened the peace and stability of the world much as had been the case with militant, militarized Fascism, and that it was up to us, newly emerged as a superpower, to heed the lessons of the past and turn back its sorties with whatever force was called for—to behave, in short, as the democracies of Europe had not behaved when threatened by Nazi Germany a decade earlier. Though we had demobilized with a haste that disheartened many of our allies, the use of force in what we regarded as a just cause did not seem offensive to us, and when the Republic of Korea— our ward and that of the United Nations—was the victim of armed attack, we rearmed.

In the hundred years that followed the close of the Civil War in 1865, ours was a reasonably—in some ways uncommonly—stable society. We and our institutions changed in many ways, but the change was almost always orderly, which is what is meant by stability. What divided us was seldom ideological, and seldom was there any great distance between what passed for the "extremes" of opinion. It may be possible to exaggerate the changes that have come in the last twenty years; it may be that at least a mathematical majority continues to adhere to the general consensus described above. But the trend has been toward quite radical changes in attitudes, toward wider differences and divisions, and toward a great increase in the numbers who dissent from the consensus. Our crusading zeal has ebbed; affluence, much of it spent on education, has been accompanied by a heightening sophistication about the world and its affairs and by a spreading skepticism and disenchantment with our political system and our public institutions. In the middle class, which spawns dissenters and is despised by them, there has developed a new and strange hedonism that particularly and peculiarly afflicts the young. We are not, I think, a more attractive people than we were —rather, the contrary—but we are in many ways less self-righteous. Both the best and the worst spirits among us are turning inward more than they were before, given more to seeking individual grace and salvation—the consequences being, on the one hand, an admirable willingness to work and sacrifice on behalf of the disadvantaged and, on the other hand, a less admirable self-indulgence that increases

[ 28 ]

the demand for everything from drugs to yachts and sports cars, from unrestricted sexual license to the right to behave as irresponsibly and obnoxiously as underdeveloped consciences may dictate.

The difference between the two periods was well stated by Richard F. Babcock, a Chicago attorney, in a letter written two years ago to an influential newspaper columnist. After describing what seemed to him the parallels between Korea and Vietnam, he wrote:

There is, then, little difference, morally, strategically, or politically, between Korea in 1950 and Vietnam in 1966. Yet the first was and still is regarded as a demonstration of American moral stamina at its best, the latter as a moral and strategic aberration.

The difference, I suspect, is that we are at 1966 and not 1950. There is, for example, a temporal relation between the domestic civil rights struggle and Vietnam. The student who protests both racial discrimination and Vietnam is not irresponsible in his motivations—he is consistent. We are in an era of incredible affluence and, consequently, of sensitive national conscience in matters not only domestic but foreign. We are a generation away from World War II. Korea had no Watts. Korea was, however, only five years from Nuremberg and at the doorstep of McCarthy.

This historical setting, it seems to me, is the key. And if so, it suggests that responsible critics do a disservice to the country when they fail to point out that Vietnam suffers not from a failure to come up to a moral or strategic imperative but that it takes place at a time when America is in a period of self-appraisal absent in 1950.

Perhaps we make more than we should of affluence as an agent of change. I tend to think it has been of enormous importance in determining the character of dissent (the "dropout" mentality of the hippies is possible only when the alternative is material comfort and a general complacency), but it is well to bear in mind that the last great upsurge of pacifism and protest in our history was in the depths of the last great depression. Dissent was then, as now, associated with youth and directed against war (the distant threat of war at that) and social injustice. But a spirit of dissent was growing in the late Eisenhower years, when our commitment in Vietnam, though already deep and dangerous, involved very few people and was known to few. It was to some extent reaction to racial injustice and poverty; it was no less, I think, a response to the drab, dispiriting rule of the affluent in the closing years of the Eisenhower administration. There had been considerable social and intellectual ferment in the late fifties, and it played a part in the election in 1960 of John F. Kennedy, whose extraordinary campaign was an attack on the complacency of his countrymen—exactly that complacency that

Eisenhower had exploited in two successful campaigns—and a call not just for new management of the country's affairs but for new values for the whole of American society. It cannot be said that the society made the kind of response that might most have gratified Kennedy, who became President with less than a popular majority and would certainly have lost if Eisenhower had been able to run again, but his election was evidence of change and his brief Presidency the occasion for more change. The nation that mourned Kennedy in 1963 and elected Johnson in 1964 was very different from the one that had chosen Dwight Eisenhower's leadership in 1952.

In 1968, 1964 seems decades in the past. A mere four years ago, we were more nearly a united people than we had ever been in this century; today we seem in an advanced state of disintegration. We are so deeply divided as a people that to many of us the divisions alone seem sufficient cause for disengaging in Vietnam even if to do so exposes us to new dangers abroad and to new and painful confrontations here at home. Yet the major changes had largely been accomplished by 1964. Given a preview of what was about to happen in Vietnam, any observer of American affairs might have anticipated the divisions of 1968 by a study of the consensus of

1964 and of the coalition that in that year elected Johnson by an unprecedented majority. What counted most against Johnson's opponent then was his loose talk of escalation in Vietnam. Goldwater's militant anti-Communism, almost an official creed ten years earlier, had become attractive only to the far right. We favored a negotiated end to the Cold War. There was not then much violence in the ghettos, but there was growing anger in the Negro community, and its consequences had been prophetically described by James Baldwin, whose *The Fire Next Time* had appeared in 1962. In 1964 it was possible to believe that there need be no "fire" because there need be no "next time." Vietnam has dashed that belief and the hope it held, not for all time, perhaps, but probably for our time. What distresses us so in 1968 is that we find ourselves playing a role that was repugnant to the people we had become by 1964.

It is often said that the prevalence of television, which came into our lives along with the Cold War, has done much to shape our attitudes toward such phenomena as war, racial injustice, and violence, and to the personalities of public men. It would be surprising if this were not to a large extent so. The war in Vietnam is close to the center of the national consciousness because of the ease with which we can "follow" it—"live," or almost so—on television. Because of television, it is impossible to be unaware of, and hence indifferent to, the war, as the people of the European colonial powers in the eighteenth and nineteenth centuries were largely unaware of the prolonged and costly campaigns—many of them much like the war in Vietnam—being carried on by their armies and navies in distant parts of the world. I also think it likely that, as some people believe, the daily cocktail-time spectacle of death and atrocity (I sat down to dinner not long ago just as CBS was showing some American troops cutting the ears off Vietcong corpses as souvenirs of the combat) has contributed to the spreading revulsion and to anti-war sentiment.

To argue this case, however, it would seem necessary to explain how it happens that a people with an enormous appetite for violence on television, in movies, and in highbrow as much as in low- and middlebrow literature may be repelled by a few minutes a day of the real thing, which is very often less sickening than the simulated variety. This would be no problem for Norman Mailer or H. Rap Brown, each of whom tells us that we are and always have been a violent people and that the televised war in Vietnam satisfies our lust for violence and serves as a graduate school in murder for our young men. I reject this view. Despite our lynchings, gang wars, race riots, and casual military undertakings, I do not think our people are particularly given to violence. They are human beings and have their share of human weaknesses, of which a lust for violence has always been one. If violence is as American as apple pie, it is also as French as *quiche Lorraine*. The French wars in Indochina and Algeria were conducted more savagely than ours in Vietnam. I am not sure that a Negro at the mercy of the police in Birmingham, Alabama, would be any worse off than a Frenchman at the mercy of the *gendarmerie* of Marseilles. There have been as many attempts on the life of Charles de Gaulle as on the lives of all American Presidents put together. The British, an uncommonly homogeneous people, are an orderly lot in their island home, but on their distant frontiers—in Australia, in East Africa, in India—they have been as violent as Americans ever were in Texas, Oklahoma, or New Mexico. I have been in many parts of the world where violence, organized and unorganized, is far more easily provoked than as a rule it is here and far more a part of everyday existence.

I do not know why our popular culture is so hung up on violence and sadism. I think it may have less to do with the popularity of violence than with the popularity, or third-rateness, of the culture and with the kind of talent that turns out all this awful stuff. That is to say, a partial explanation may be that violence, like sentimentality, lends itself to easy exploitation. A stupid or lazy dramatist can save himself a lot of hard work by writing scenes in which the action consists of people maiming one another. An exchange of gunfire can be more easily and convincingly dramatized than a clash of human will. And, of course, people go for it—but not just Americans. Ours is a culture largely manufactured for export, and the very worst of it is a smash hit all over the world. But just as the carnality of our popular culture does not prove that we are more libidinous than others, its emphasis on violence does not prove that we are more brutish than others.

Furthermore, there is to be observed an almost complete disjuncture between the violence of Vietnam and the violence of our cinematic and electronic fantasies. Although war movies like *The Dirty Dozen* are big at the box office, the most topical of wars, Vietnam, has yet to be the subject of a motion picture. This, we are told on excellent authority, is not because the producers are reluctant to exploit it. The subject has been deliberately avoided, it seems, for reasons rather like those behind the avoidance— at least, until recently—of the subjects of sodomy and miscegenation. It would offend the audience, or a good part of it, and in acknowledgment of this fact—presumably established by the usual market surveys—the major producers have agreed among themselves to lay off. Even as heady a matching of star and subject as John Wayne and the Army Special Forces has had difficulty attracting the capital needed for a picture to be called *The Green Berets*. If, à la Norman Mailer, President Johnson is only John Wayne in the White House, he may be more vulnerable than we know.

As a nation among nations, as a force in the world, we may be behaving more chauvinistically today than we have ever behaved in the past. This almost has to be true, because our power is so immense that any ugly display of it makes an impression commensurate with its magnitude. But among us, as a people, chauvinism and jingoism have been declining steadily since the First World War. Although Hitler's Germany was more detestable than Kaiser Wilhelm's, there was less Hun-hating in the Second World War than in the First. What was "liberty cabbage" in 1918 was sauerkraut in 1945. There was not much flag-waving in the Second World War, and still less in the Korean war. But now we seem to have made a really radical break with the past. This is the first war of the century of which it is true that opposition to it is not only widespread but fashionable. It is the first in connection with which it seems in downright bad taste to invoke patriotism; while the Korean war was still in progress, theaters were showing such movies about it as *A Yank in Korea, Korea Patrol, Glory Brigade, Battle Circus,* and *Mission Over Korea.* In the two wars before this one, there was a conspicuous shortage of martial airs; and now, for the first time, popular songs of bitter protest, such as Joan Baez's "Saigon Bride" and Pete Seeger's "Waist Deep in the Big Muddy," are part of the popular culture.

If we could gauge a nation's penchant for violence by its official rhetoric and its popular culture, China would stand first in both categories. In the rhetoric department, we would rank far down the list, and in popular culture, perhaps second or third, though it is not to be forgotten that many others consume our product exactly as we do. Some Chinese are behaving very strangely of late, but I do not for a moment believe they are an abnormally violent people, and I am not so sure their leaders are more violent than ours. They just talk rougher and beat more people up. The medium is not the message. The message I get from my eyes and ears is that because of this war and certain attendant miseries, kookiness of every sort is alarmingly on the rise. At the same time, if it's a sign of sanity to be against the war, and a sign of relative sanity to prefer a limited war to the world's last great shoot-out, we are in better shape than many of us know. Consider the extraordinary extent of the opposition to this war—and, perhaps equally notable, the distaste for the war among those who do not oppose it. Nothing like this has been known in this century. Ordinarily, in this and most other modern states, opposition to war evaporates once the decision to wage it has been taken, once the killing has begun. When the bugles sound and the colors are unfurled, almost everyone becomes a patriot of the Stephen Decatur, or my-country-right-or-wrong, persuasion. Such patriots seem very scarce today, and they speak softly, if at all. In the Senate there are a handful of screaming eagles, but mostly there are old-school politicians—like Senator Richard Russell, of Georgia—who explain in patient, weary voices that we have to get on with the war because, regardless of the merits of the enterprise, we are in it and have committed our troops and our honor to it. Here is a terse description of the extraordinary state of affairs in the United States Senate in late 1967—a summary, by CBS, of a survey it conducted.

On Vietnam, the U.S. Senate is advising more and consenting less. In the CBS News survey, nearly half the senators responding said they disapproved the conduct of the war. Open support for the Gulf of Tonkin resolution dropped dramatically. Eighteen senators wanted the bombing of North Vietnam completely stopped.

We talked with 95 senators. Eight of them refused to participate, 87 responding to the questions on the conduct of the war. Three years ago, President Johnson took a survey of his own. It was called the Gulf of Tonkin resolution, supporting his authority to do anything necessary in Southeast Asia. Eighty-eight approved then, two did not. Today, only 34 are prepared to publicly support a Tonkin resolution without reservation or change. Fifteen refused to comment, and where two voted against it in 1964, 20 would now vote no.

On Vietnam today, 42 senators disapprove the administration's conduct of the war. Thirty-two approve. Eleven would not commit themselves, including the Senate's minority leader, Everett Dirksen. His "no comment" follows strong defense of the President on the floor. Disapproval takes two directions. Fifteen are dissatisfied because they want more military action to end the war. Twenty-seven want less, in the form of bombing pauses or de-escalations.

Most senators feel their constituents think as they do, 46 reporting the folks at home disapprove the handling of the war, 22 reporting constituent approval. They notice a recent change in their public's opinion, too. Thirty-three of the senators say their people have shifted, and 28 of them say it is in the direction wanting less military action.

On bombing policy, the Senate goes in all directions. Eighteen want bombing of the North completely stopped. Twenty-one say it should be increased, to include more lucrative targets. Twenty-four go along with whatever the President or the military want to do, and 12 suggest less bombing or a pause.

The sleeper question of the survey turned out to be the last one, asking if the senators favored direct negotiations with the Vietcong. There was more agreement on this than anything else. Forty-six senators said yes. Sixteen said no to direct talks with the guerrilla front. One of them wanted a military victory so complete as to have no Vietcong left to negotiate with.

Many answers to the CBS News survey were qualified, justifying the opinion of several senators that polls never really satisfy with a full measure of attitudes, but three things do emerge: a crumbling of the solid front support given three years ago with the Gulf of Tonkin resolution, an infectious restlessness in the Senate and among its constituents with the progress of the war, and a growing impatience with a long twilight struggle where victories do not decide, and the end cannot be seen.

Whether or not they mean it, the leaders of the administration miss no opportunity to wring their hands and insist that it is peace, and not victory, they seek, and that they are ready at any time to sit down with anyone anywhere, and so on. ("I would depart today for any mutually convenient spot," Rusk says, "if I could meet a representative of North Vietnam with whom I could discuss peace in Southeast Asia.") *Do* they mean it? Who knows? If they don't mean it, why are they saying it? If they didn't talk so much, the credibility gap might narrow. But they go on. Week after week in the fall of 1967, the Secretary of Defense, the master of the greatest war machine in history, seemed to be trying to signal to us, his countrymen, that the damned thing wasn't working, that the bombing was pointless, that it should be stopped. Did he speak for the President? Evidently not, yet he held the job during that period. As for the President, speaking of mankind's behavior in this century, he said in October 1967, in Williamsburg, Virginia, "We can take no pride in the fact that we have fought each other like animals." He added that it "is really an insult to the animals, who live together in more harmony than human beings seem to be able to do." After some generalizations on other failures of statesmanship, he said, "Shame on the world and shame on its leaders." Those who support the war, like those who oppose it, appeal not to the patriotic heart but to the bleeding one. This is without precedent.

Consider, also, the attitudes toward civilian deaths, casualties, and the general human suffering brought by the war to the Vietnamese, North and South. These, too, are without known precedent. Whether this war is like or unlike any earlier one, it resembles all modern wars in that noncombatants are killed, the innocent suffer greatly, and there is much cruel and needless destruction. In Korea, we bombed and shelled villages, killed countless women and children. No Senate committees pestered the generals to learn how many civilians had been killed or what steps were being taken to avoid the slaughter of the innocents. *C'est la guerre.* We killed a great many civilians, some with napalm, in the Second World War. If they were Germans or Japanese, it served them right. (Hiroshima produced some immediate revulsion, but it was the newness and hideousness of the weapon employed that affected us, who had been little moved by wider killing with mere TNT.) If they were Italians or Frenchmen, we thought of their deaths as gallant sacrifices they made happily for the liberation of their soil. To be sure, civilized people have always felt that noncombatants should be spared to the greatest extent consistent with military needs, but until now there was no doubt in anyone's mind that the military needs—provided, of course, they were our own—should be the first consideration. Any sense of outrage over atrocities and dead civilians was directed at the enemy. Now, for the first time, the conscience of a large part of the nation has been aroused by agonies for which our own forces are responsible.

All wars are brutalizing, and perhaps in the random violence of the past few years (not merely the riots—not even so much the riots as the murders and assassinations) we are paying part of the price for sanctioned murder in the name of anti-Communism, self-determination, and democracy. But what seems already clear—from the size of the antiwar movements, from the muting of the eagles, from the outrage over atrocities and civilian losses—is that there is building up in this country a powerful sentiment not simply against the war in Vietnam but against war itself, not simply against bombing in Vietnam but against bombing anywhere at any time for any reason, not simply against the slaughter of innocents in an unjust conflict but also against the slaughter of those who may be far from innocent in a just conflict. The youthful protesters would probably acknowledge this without hesitation, only asking themselves why anyone should labor the point so heavily. (Some would no doubt go further, and say that they oppose not only the wars this government runs but everything else it does.) Their elders, thinking of a past they find it necessary to be true to, cannot turn pacifist overnight. They must distinguish between this war and wars they have supported in the past—up to and including the war in the Middle East less than a year ago. But in fact our present war is different mainly in that it seems endless and hopeless and irrelevant to the felt needs of mankind today.

Is it possible for us to come through this experience, if we come through at all, as a pacifist nation? I suppose not. "Pacifist nation" seems a contradiction in terms. If all of us, or most of us, were pacifists, we would have little reason to be a nation. Defense is the fundamental *raison d'être* for the modern state. And if a pacifist nation didn't come apart at the seams, some nonpacifist nation would tear it apart. It seems to me, though, that if the war goes on and if opposition to it continues to increase at the present rate, there will in time be a testing of this whole proposition. No government that is not totalitarian can go on indefinitely fighting a hard war that its people hate. Something has to give. Either the government yields to the popular will or it becomes oppressive and stifles the protest by terror. As yet, there is no sign that our government has faced the question. With very few exceptions, as far as the antiwar movement is concerned, police power has been used sparingly and in the interests of domestic tranquillity. Few other governments, even when they were not at war, would be as restrained as this one has been in dealing with protest movements, including violent ones.

It seems to me that this is in part because at least until recently we were waging the Vietnam war with an essentially professional military force. Morale is said to be high and not to be much affected by what is going on here. This state of affairs cannot last in-definitely. Morale will be affected, and then the test will be made. I cannot figure the odds on the out-come. On the one hand, repression is the safest, surest, cheapest course for any government to take. I can imagine the coming to power of an American de Gaulle, or even of someone a lot more authoritarian than de Gaulle. Much of the troublemaking in the months and years ahead will be the work of Ne-groes, and I can even imagine the imposition of a kind of American apartheid—at least in the North, where Negroes live in ghettos that are easily sealed off. If there should be the will to do it, it could be done quite "legally" and "constitutionally." There are enough smart lawyers around to figure out how. On the other hand, there is unprecedented opposi-tion to the war inside the "power structure" itself. There is much opposition in Congress and in every department of the federal government. The gover-nors of large states and the mayors of great cities—among them the mayor of New York—are opposed to the war. The Supreme Court, which was such a bastion of liberty in the McCarthy years, would make things as hard as possible for all the smart lawyers. The government could, of course, ignore, or even abolish, the Supreme Court. But the Court is not the only American institution that has proved quite resilient in periods of stress. The churches, the press, the universities—all are centers of dissent. It could prove to be crucial that the American middle class—as despicable as the Establishment in the minds of the young and alienated—is also a center of dissent. The proletariat may not be willing to call off strikes or accept pay cuts because of the war, but it offers little support to the protest movements. If we are now undertaking, or are about to undertake, a radical alteration in values, support for this will come not from the workers but from an unproclaimed and unwanted alliance between relatively affluent whites, of whom I happen to be one, and what Daniel P. Moynihan calls the "under-class," consisting mainly of unemployed Negroes, many of whom want to kill me.

I want American democracy to survive. It is in many ways a fraud. It is not keeping its promises to American Negroes. It has abused them and many other people. It has little aesthetic or intellectual appeal. But as human societies go, this is a good one. Not more than two or three other countries come as close to the ideal of representative government as we do. We not only profess but strive to attain the ideal of universal education. And I do not scorn our material achievements; we have used our resources to bring the great mass of our people far above subsistence levels. By and large, civil liberties are secure. As an individual, I am freer here than I would be almost anywhere else on earth. And this is not because my skin is some kind of off-beige. As an individual, James Baldwin has the same rights and privileges. Civil rights, as distinct from civil liberties, are less secure. This society is, as its detractors never tire of telling us, racist. The charge impresses me no more than the accusation that we are uniquely violent. I might be impressed if someone could tell me where to find a society, in the past or in the present, that was not racist. To presume the natural superiority and superior righteousness of one's clan, tribe, and race seems to me very human—deplorably so, of course, like so much else that is human. So far as I know, ours is the first society to have made any kind of national effort to overcome racism. In some ways, we have made remarkable progress. I think we would have gone much further if it were not for this war, which not merely deflects our government's energies but, and this seems more important, alienates many of those whose own energies are greatly needed if the effort is to succeed. But under democracy there is at least a hope of redemption. Things do get done here that don't get done under other systems.

It now seems clear to me that if American democracy does survive it will be something quite different from what we have known. I find it hard at this stage to see how a victory for democracy will not also be a victory for pacifism. Those who will lead the struggle are, whether they acknowledge it or not, renouncing war as an instrument of policy. They may insist that of course they would fight the enemy at the gates, or perhaps take arms against a new Hitler if one should arise. But the wars of the future—at least, those that would have any ideological content—are not going to be like the wars of the past. India and Pakistan or India and China may fight over bits and pieces of territory, but the Soviet Union and the United States are agreed on the need for common efforts to cool it when such disputes get hot. Most future wars are apt to be like the war in Vietnam—wars that will be called by their instigators "wars of national liberation." The Soviet Union, as Nikita Khrushchev long ago informed us, will support them. From the Soviet point of view, they are irresistible. They cost next to nothing and drive us Americans out of our minds.

But if we survive as anything like a free society, we will not be entering them. I simply cannot imagine this country, under Lyndon Johnson or any other President chosen in a free election, taking on another Vietnam. Nor, it is far more important to note, can a man who may very well find himself in the White House next year, Richard M. Nixon, who, in an uncharacteristically penetrating article in *Foreign Affairs* for October 1967, wrote:

One of the legacies of Vietnam almost certainly will be a deep reluctance on the part of the United States to become involved once again in a similar intervention on a similar basis. The war has imposed severe strains on the United States, not only militarily and economically but socially and politically as well. Bitter dissension has torn the fabric of American intellectual life, and whatever the outcome of the war, the tear may be a long time mending. If another friendly country should be faced with externally supported Communist insurrection —whether in Asia or in Africa or even Latin America— there is serious question whether the American public or the American Congress would now support a unilateral American intervention, even at the request of the host government.*

---

* An incident from his own past must have been very much on the former Vice-President's mind when he wrote this. On April 16, 1954, when the French were under siege at Dienbienphu, Nixon, according to reports subsequently verified by him, told a closed session of the American Society of Newspaper Editors that we might soon be sending troops to Indochina. He was only saying what most members of the National Security Council then believed. But despite the fact that the step had the approval of the Joint Chiefs and the Secretary of State (President Eisenhower was golfing in Augusta and saying very little), it was never taken. What appears to have caused the reversal of policy was public hostility. Sounding out their constituents during the Easter recess in 1954, congressmen discovered that the memory of Korea, where we had disengaged less than a year earlier, was too fresh and too distasteful for people to accept

[ 49 ]

If Nixon and I are right, we may be bearers of good news. But let it be clear that we are talking about a return to isolationism. We will draw back from difficult situations and leave the field to those who have not renounced war.

---

another Asian adventure. In the end, the President put his foot down. "The President knew that the American people had no appetite for another war [in] Asia," Sherman Adams wrote in his 1961 memoir, *Firsthand Report*.

# III

# A New Situation
# in the World

In 1948, when he was Secretary of State and putting in place the foundation stones of postwar American foreign policy, General Marshall was asked to describe his objective. What was the United States hoping to accomplish in the world? How and when would we know whether or not we had succeeded? The Secretary said he could not answer a question put in these terms. He supposed that what we were really trying to do was to buy time for ourselves and the world, to avoid the kind of confrontation with the Soviet Union that the whole world—or at any rate the whole Western world—dreaded. He was then asked if the mere postponement of conflict was a suitably large and noble aim for this great and powerful democracy. It would not be, he said, if it

were merely a matter of putting off the inevitable—
of stalling long enough to pass an irreconcilable conflict on to another generation. But he did not, he
said, see it in quite that light. He was not certain
that the conflict would always be as irreconcilable as
it then appeared to be. In his reading of history, the
world and its problems took on a new appearance
every twenty or thirty years—the span of a generation—and what might seem an insoluble problem in
1948 might by 1968 or 1978 seem quite amenable
to solutions undreamed by the generation that had
no strategy better than delay. The problem might
even disappear completely in such a period—as, on
the other hand, it might loom larger than ever. He
said, as John Bartlow Martin has it in *Overtaken by
Events,* that "if we could just hold on for twenty or
thirty years without starting a nuclear war, we could
be sure of one thing and one thing only: the world
would be a different place."*

----

* This is a paraphrase by Martin, not a quotation from
Marshall. I can cite no source but memory—my own and
that of a few others—for Marshall's observations, and my
memory does not retain the date or the occasion for them.
I am not altogether sure I am right in giving the year as
1948—it could have been 1947 or 1949. But it was during
his tenure as Secretary of State. I was impressed—and, as
I recall, somewhat depressed—at the time and the thought
has stayed with me through the years. I was more depressed
than impressed, however, when I came upon an echo of
Marshall in the pages of *Life* for December 1, 1967. In an
article about W. W. Rostow, the most "hawkish" of the
President's advisers on Vietnam, Rostow was quoted as saying, "The duty of men is to prevent war and buy time."

Marshall's rationale for American policy was never embodied in any official proclamation, never made part of any "doctrine." Although it accords with a view of life and history that has been part of our culture from Solomon ("Our time is a very shadow that passes away") to Mr. Justice Holmes ("Time has upset many fighting faiths"), it is, for politicians seeking votes from the electorate and funds from the Congress, a vulnerable and unsatisfactory way of looking at the world. It can be attacked as being either bleakly pessimistic or irresponsibly Micawberish. It lacks moral grandeur and provides a rather insubstantial foundation for the building of a national morale. Nevertheless, it has for many years seemed to me to embody the only intellectually honest and humane approach that can be made to the crucial issues of diplomacy in an age of great and potentially explosive international rivalries. We can, perhaps, "plan" for such things as the political and economic development of Latin America and Africa with reasonable confidence that people whose basic human needs are being met and who are more or less in control of their own destinies will have a stake in an orderly world. Theoretically, we can also plan, by means of alliances and the development of our own internal strength, to create a world balance of power favorable to us (or a world balance of terror not *un*favorable to us), but it is all at best a gamble on the future and on the changes that, for better or worse, are bound to come with the passage of time. But even with the balance of power heavily in our favor, our safety and survival are never assured. We can never presume rationality as a determining factor in the life of mankind.

But we cannot presume irrationality either—not without being untrue to our culture and to the best of our experience. And although what is different is not necessarily better and may often be worse, we know from certain of our travails that there are things that men can do to bring a measure of order into the world and to induce those bent on irrational courses to abandon or alter them. Not to try them is to resign ourselves to chaos and possible extinction. In any event, Marshall's view of the aim of policy seems to me to provide a sounder guide to the present and to the recent past than any that has been offered by those haggling over the meaning and wisdom of "self-determination" and "containment."

Marshall thought that the world would be a different place a generation later. The time has passed, and the world is so very different that fathers cannot convince grown sons, young men born into that other world, that the place ever existed and that its terrors were real. Neither the offender nor the offended is the same. Though Lyndon Johnson may in certain respects put one in mind of Harry Truman, the United States of 1968 is very different from the United States of 1948. We have become a different people, some of us who recall 1948 being terribly estranged from our former selves. Our society has a different structure, different values, different aims. What is true of us seems in some ways even more true of our 1948 adversaries. More important to what is under consideration here, our relationships have been radically altered. What we once thought of as the Cold War, essentially a contest for political influence in Western Europe, has for all practical purposes been settled. The cockpits now are Southeast Asia and the Middle East. But the rivalries in those places are much more complex, partly because of enormous changes that have taken place in what was once called "the Communist world." If it ever existed, that world is now dead. Communism is scarcely more binding ideologically than monarchy or democracy.

We are, I would suggest, in trouble today not because we have changed our policies but because we have failed to do so. The policies we are applying were meant not for perpetuity but merely to tide us over, to bring us safely into the present age. We have arrived, and it has become incumbent upon us to look upon this new age and seek new ways—if new ways are required, and it seems to me perfectly clear that they are most desperately required—of dealing with it. Instead, our leaders and many of their most eloquent critics are locked in debate over who is and who is not being true to a bygone age.

The world has changed even in what we mean when we speak of it. Although, as noted, there has been an American presence in Asia for the better part of a century, although we had just dismantled Japan's Greater East Asia Co-Prosperity Sphere, and although we were shortly to intervene in Korea, the hopes and fears of the late forties turned almost exclusively on Europe. When Marshall spoke of avoiding war, he meant war on the mainland of Europe—on the very territories of Germany, France, the Low Countries, and Italy that were yet to be cleared of the rubble of World War II. As he spoke, civil war raged in China and in many other parts of the world, but what was feared in this country was a war with the Soviet Union to prevent its doing in the late forties what Nazi Germany had done in the early forties. That was the fear. The hope was that this country and its allies could deter the Soviet Union by building the kind of collective security system that, had it existed ten years earlier, might have spared the world the war of 1939–1945.

There are now historians who maintain that our fears of twenty years ago were not grounded in reality or logic and that such tensions as existed were mainly of Western fabrication. I do not now wish to get into this controversy; it is not particularly relevant to my present concerns. Looking westward from the Kremlin, Stalin and his associates, men who had lately suffered much and who had themselves caused much suffering, may well have felt justified in concluding that American power—augmented by nuclear weapons, which they did not then possess— threatened Soviet sovereignty. It may also be that regardless of who or what started the Cold War, our response to its real or imagined challenges was a woefully mistaken one; if it could someday be argued, by insect survivors of the holocaust, that the Truman Doctrine and the Marshall Plan had led directly to nuclear war with the Soviet Union and/ or China and thence to the end of mankind, there would be a strong prima facie case against our whole postwar policy. Still, we must deal with the human perceptions that men rely on when they attempt to determine their lives. The Soviet Union that emerged from the war in 1945 was as totalitarian as Hitler's Germany had ever been. In our need, we had collaborated with it. We were prepared to go on doing so, provided it did not attempt

to spread its power far beyond its prewar boundaries. We were prepared to accept a Soviet sphere of
influence in Eastern Europe. It had been established
well before the end of the war. George Kennan, then
in the Moscow embassy, had proposed in 1944 that
American military and economic aid be cut off immediately on the ground that the Soviets had turned
a war *against* aggression into a war *of* aggression in
Eastern Europe, but the suggestion was unaccepta-
ble in Washington, and although we muffed certain
opportunities for postwar economic cooperation, we
were nevertheless still willing in 1947 to have the
Soviets and what were then so clearly their satellites
take part in the Marshall Plan. What we were not
prepared to do was see the Soviet Union extend its
dominance to all of Europe.

That this was ever a real and serious intent in
Moscow has never been certain. To be sure, Moscow
was eager to strengthen the Communist parties in
the West—all at that time, of course, Moscow-
oriented—and would have been delighted to see
any of them seize power. But though some then
thought that the main threat to Western Europe
lay in the growth of Western Communist parties,
the liveliest fear was that the Red Army massed
along what was becoming known as the Iron Curtain
would move against the defenseless democracies. "If

[it] is accepted that the Soviet Union has a right to penetrate her immediate neighbors for security," Averell Harriman said in 1944, "penetration of the next immediate neighbors becomes at a certain time equally logical." We shall perhaps never know whether Stalin played with the possibilities of applying Harriman's logic. He did not need instruction in the cost of doing so. The United States had atomic bombs, and it would have occurred to him quite early that we could do to Moscow and Leningrad what we had done to Hiroshima and Nagasaki. Some, like Bertrand Russell, were then urging that we do exactly this, in advance of any aggression and with no greater assurances than Harriman's "logic" that aggression was being contemplated or planned.

Cooler heads prevailed. In 1968, this may be judged as rather a modest victory for rationality; a decision not to commit wanton murder or massacre is something less than a triumph of the human spirit. But in the late forties there were men of high intelligence and a morality not less estimable than Lord Russell's who felt that restraint might be a form of suicide. Some thought that the only way to spare the world a vastly more destructive war than the one against Hitler was to threaten Moscow with the use of American nuclear weapons, and if the threat was ignored and Russian armies remained menacingly deployed in Eastern Europe, destroy the Soviet regime with dispatch. We had a nuclear monopoly for more than four years. It was no secret that the Russians were on their way to breaking it. Throughout the West, it was assumed that when we no longer had a monopoly, the Soviets would have no scruples about using nuclear weapons and, later, thermonuclear ones, which were clearly in the offing as and when it seemed advantageous to do so. In February 1949, seven months before the Atomic Energy Commission confirmed the detonation of an atomic device in the Soviet Union, President Truman said to David E. Lilienthal, chairman of the commission, "Dave, we will never use it again if we can help it. But I know the Russians would use it against us if they had it." They got it, and they have yet to use it—though we can only speculate as to what might have happened if they, rather than we, had ever been in a position to destroy without being destroyed. Communism at the time was monolithic and messianic; the Soviet Union had not emulated us in hasty demobilization; it had already used force for conquest; its diplomacy was everywhere disruptive and threatening. And so something more than smugness and a simplistic anti-Communism made "preventive war" or "pre-emptive strikes" subjects for grave consideration not only for short-fused jingos but for sober scientists like Harold Urey and Leo Szilard and for humane statesmen here and in many other countries. "If we are *sure* to have a world war," Leo Szilard said in 1945, "the later it comes, the worse for us." In his journal for April 1, 1949, Lilienthal wrote of an evening spent with Senator Brien McMahon of Connecticut, a circumspect man who served as chairman of the Joint Congressional Committee on Atomic Energy and who was as knowledgeable as anyone in Washington, Lilienthal excepted, on nuclear politics and diplomacy: "What he is talking about is the inevitability of war with the Russians and what he says adds up to one thing: blow them off the face of the earth, quick, before they do the same to us."

McMahon did not make public his despair or urge a policy based upon it. Nor, though many shared it, did any other important figures in the government. No assumption of the inevitability of anything underlay our policy then or in the years that followed. Hope was based on the beneficent workings of time, and the effort to buy it commenced. The alternative to war was "containment"—justified by the hope that time might show Mr. Justice Holmes right about "fighting faiths" and George Kennan sound in anticipating the "breakup or the gradual mellowing" of Soviet power. The Truman Doctrine was proclaimed; the Marshall Plan was drawn up; and, in time, NATO, the containing force, was organized. Despite the deplorably loose wording of the Truman Doctrine, which could be and was read as an announcement that the United States would henceforth render assistance to any countries anywhere that were "resisting subjugation by armed minorities or by outside pressures," these and all other measures undertaken in the late forties were designed for the purpose of enabling Western Europe to live and seek economic recovery in a state of what Stalin was to call "peaceful coexistence" with the Soviets and what could then be legitimately regarded as their occupied colonies to the east.

I might add, parenthetically, that the danger of such an open-ended commitment was quickly perceived. Dean Acheson, then Under-Secretary of State, tried immediately to disabuse anyone who might suppose that the Truman Doctrine meant unquestioning assistance for any country in any kind of trouble. On March 14, 1947, in testimony before the Senate Foreign Relations Committee, he said: "It cannot be assumed that this government would necessarily undertake measures in any other country identical or even closely similar to those proposed for Greece and Turkey." He had no stomach for policing the world. Indeed, it strikes me that the reason the language was so lacking in specificity was that the framers of it were so strongly Europe-oriented in their thinking that they were unaware of any need to qualify. Europe and the "world" were still pretty much one. The great empires were for the most part still intact. Despite our disapproval of them, we had no choice but to deal with them as they were and to regard Indochina, say, as part of France, with most of Africa and much of Asia as dependencies of one or another of the European powers. The explosion of new sovereignties that has brought United Nations membership to 122 was more than a decade away. In a sense, the world of 1948 *was* Europe.

In our preoccupation with Vietnam in 1968, we are likely to think of the wretched war there as the only foreign policy we have. Unhappily it comes closer and closer to being that, but it remains for the present true that we are engaged—peaceably for the most part and in some places usefully—in many other places in the world. Similarly, it would be mistaken to convey the impression that our *only* concern two decades ago was with the future of Western Europe. The occupation of Japan was no small enterprise. Efforts were being made by General Marshall and others to end the civil war in China. We recognized the state of Israel and supported its right to sovereignty. We applied considerable leverage against the European colonial powers to divest themselves of their holdings in Asia. In 1948, we led in the formation of the Organization of American States in Bogotá. In 1949, Truman announced the Point Four Program, the modest beginning of American technical aid to underdeveloped countries. And of course there was support for the United Nations, for which there were great expectations born partly of our own messianic impulses, never to be taken lightly in any consideration of our role in the world, and partly of our guilt for having failed Woodrow Wilson in 1919.

As the forties gave way to the fifties and the Democrats to the Republicans, our involvements outside Europe began to increase. Our role as an occupying power and our eagerness to make the U.N. work had much to do with our intervention in Korea—as did the hardening of anti-Communism as a national ideology and our fear of Soviet expansionism. John Foster Dulles raised anti-Communism from ideology to theology. Moreover, he was the first true globalist to become Secretary of State. He did not complain of the lack of specificity in the Truman Doctrine. He wanted us to smite the devil everywhere—or so at least he said—even in those provinces, such as the satellite states of Eastern Europe, where Satan's rule had been a *fait accompli* for several years. He traveled the world like a possessed insurance salesman, offering bargains in American protection to any nation whose leaders would give him their word that they, too, despised Communism.

Still and all, it was Europe that really worried us, the Europe that most of us came from, the Europe that twice in a quarter-century had drawn our armies across the Atlantic. We had no fear of Japan rising again. Korea was a nasty experience, but neither before it nor for several years after it did we have any fear that we might be drawn into a major war with China. We lobbied for the independence of India and for the liquidation of the Dutch and French empires in Asia not because we saw any deep involvement of the national interest in these matters but because to do otherwise would have been to dishonor our tradition and expose our pretensions as evangels of self-determination. But through it all the main thrust of our policy was in Europe. Rightly or wrongly, the Soviet Union was to us the new Germany, Stalin the new Kaiser, the new Hitler, the new threat to Europe's peace and to our own.

In the late forties I shared the anxieties of the leaders of this government about the future of Europe, and so did most of my contemporaries, including the great majority of those who now oppose the war in Vietnam. Though I now have misgivings about some things the government did, I continue to think that the anxieties were for the most part justified ones, and that given the limitations imposed on us by our humanity and given the weaknesses of our political institutions, we did not do badly. But it matters little to my present argument whether or not the dangers were real or merely apparent. What matters is that they were seen as real and that we attempted to deal with them by means of certain policies intended not to alter in any radical way the existing balance of power but to preserve it in the hope that time would produce either a solution not presently available or a new situation in the world.*

---

* As noted above, in the Eisenhower years, particularly in the early ones, the policy sometimes seemed more doctrinaire, more impatient, more militant, more directed toward change. But the difference was mainly one of rhetoric. Dulles spoke often of "liberation," of "massive retaliation," of "agonizing reappraisal," and he may have meant every word of it. But he was Secretary of State, not President, and Eisenhower, though something of a dogmatist in his views on such matters as morality and economics, was essentially pragmatic in international relations. Also, there is reason to think that Dulles was never as reckless as he sometimes sounded. The 1956 revolt in Hungary provided this country with an opportunity to engage the devil in hell itself. Eisenhower may have held Dulles in check, but if this is what happened, Dulles was never known to complain about it.

Reporting to the *New Yorker* from Washington on January 20, 1955, I wrote that "wherever there is talk of foreign policy these days, the air is electric with a sense of change. There is an almost universal feeling that the world the United States confronts today—the whole complex of political, economic, military and technological realities that constitute the environment in which the national interest must be pursued—is radically different from the world it confronted even as recently as last summer." My report went on: "Russian achievements in weapons research and development have brought into being a new power relationship between this country and the Soviet Union. Last year's hydrogen bomb experiments at the Pacific proving grounds have led to a new view of the meaning that any future resort to war would have for human life and civilization. The emergence of a new style, if not a new character, in Soviet diplomacy has created [for American diplomacy] difficulties as novel and as formidable as those that might be created by the sudden emergence of a new adversary."

Perhaps the most momentous changes in the world for which our policy was originally planned came to pass—or at least came to light—in 1955. By then, both the United States and the Soviet Union were capable and more than capable of destroying one another and the world. Very shortly, it was then clear, there would be intercontinental ballistic missiles, against which there would be no defense. War between nuclear powers had become something that no government that wished anything other than death could consider as a means of fulfilling any of its aims. This, to be sure, had been so for some time. In 1953, Joseph Stalin's successor, Georgi Malenkov, had said that "with the existence of modern weapons of destruction . . . [war] would mean the destruction of world civilization." In 1954, President Eisenhower had told a meeting of State Department officers that "since the advent of nuclear weapons, it seems clear that there is no longer any alternative to peace." But 1955 was the year in which governments hostile to one another publicly acknowledged the existence of a wholly new situation and their determination to base policy upon it.

In July 1955, the heads of government of the United States, the Soviet Union, the United Kingdom, and France foregathered in Geneva for what the Swiss called the Conférence à Quatre. The world had been led to expect much of their deliberations. It was the first "summit" meeting since the one a decade earlier at Potsdam, where the whole cast of characters had been different. The main subject on the agenda was German reunification, and to everyone's great relief nothing was done about it. "The time is not ripe for unification," said Nikolai Bulganin, who then shared leadership with Nikita Khrushchev as Alexei Kosygin now shares it with Leonid Brezhnev. No one else thought the time was ripe, either, and the world was pleased that there could be even a negative agreement. It was pleased, too, that the summiteers could sit down and discuss their differences without threats or ultimata or any grave discourtesy. For a while after the meeting, there was much speechifying and editorializing about the "spirit of Geneva" and the détente, the easing of tensions that accompanied it. But well before the year was out, disillusionment set in everywhere in the West. It had developed that even as the summiteers had been talking in Geneva, Czech and Soviet agents had been at work in Egypt offering arms to Colonel Gamal Abdel Nasser and that Moscow had been casing the entire Middle East in hopes of establishing Soviet influence throughout the region. When this was revealed, there was a tendency in most quarters to regard Geneva as nothing more than a cover for Communist duplicity. Although the Russians kept pressing for more summit meetings, it was another five years before we would consent to one.*

---

* This was the summit that never took place in Paris in June 1960. Just as the final preparations were being made, one of our U-2 spy planes was brought down by Soviet arms deep inside the Soviet Union. Eisenhower took responsibility

I have always felt that the Conférence à Quatre was an event of enormous significance. No agreements of any substance came out of it, and the Soviets probably did use it to distract the world's attention from the first steps in their Middle East adventures. Nevertheless, it was the occasion on which we and our adversaries came to an understanding that under no circumstances should our rivalries be carried to the point at which one side or the other had no alternative but war. On his way back to Moscow from Geneva, Khrushchev stopped in East Berlin and announced that "neither side wants war." This was no mere statement of the obvious; it was an admonition to Walter Ulbricht's followers to cool it, an announcement that provocations must be kept within limits. It was also a notable break with established doctrine; it is not easy for a Communist leader to tell a Communist audience that the capitalist world means it no harm. Somewhat later, addressing the Indian Parliament at New Delhi, Bulganin said that the Soviet Union "resolutely repudiates war as a means of settling international problems." It was not long before Khrushchev retired Bulganin and qualified the re-

for the mission but would not make the kind of apologies Khrushchev demanded of him. Though the conferees all reached Paris, they never conferred.

pudiation by saying that "wars of national liberation" would be regarded as an exception. For all of
that, there has been little doubt since Geneva that
neither the Soviet Union nor the United States
regarded war as an acceptable instrument of policy.

This, of course, did not eliminate the danger.
Seven years after Geneva, there was the Cuban missile crisis. A continuing source of danger lay in the
very existence of the weapons. The most exemplary
of statesmen can miscalculate. Exemplary statesmen
can be replaced by lunatics. Nations themselves can
go mad. Still, as Thomas C. Hennings, Jr., a senator
from Missouri and as perceptive a man as could then
be found in public life, had observed a few months
before the Conférence à Quartre, "the whole context
of history [has] been altered . . . None of yester-
day's assumptions can go unchallenged today." The
deterrent to war was no longer the American nuclear
capacity. Nor was it the conventional power of
NATO. The deterrent had become what Winston
Churchill called "the universality of potential destruction"—a far superior deterrent, he said, one "to
which we may look with hope and even confidence."
This meant, among other things, that the United
States would be effectively deterred as the Soviet
Union had been a few years earlier. No sane person

could any longer entertain thoughts of preventive war, since war could "prevent" nothing except the continued existence of human life. "Better Red than dead" became a self-evident proposition, though not a particularly relevant posing of available alternatives.

Both the United States and the Soviet Union made certain adaptations to the new realities. One of theirs was the move into the Middle East, more or less a non-nuclear zone. One of ours was the Central Treaty Organization, which soon ended the Middle East's non-nuclear status. But not all was tit for tat. There was mutual understanding about the reunification of Germany—they would restrain their Germans and we would restrain ours. Disarmament plans came from both sides. In the 1956 Presidential campaign, Adlai Stevenson proposed an end to nuclear testing. The proposal was denounced and Stevenson lost, but the idea gained in favor, and there were voluntary suspensions and in 1963 the Test Ban Treaty. There was, too, a realization that having put most of our efforts into weapons that were useful only in their uselessness, we had in effect disarmed ourselves and had no practical means of defending American interests; this led to a call for the reconstitution of conventional forces, which was undertaken in the late Eisenhower and early Kennedy years.

But this about exhausts the catalogue of responses on both sides. In less than a decade, the apparent danger our policy had been designed to avert—a war with the Soviet Union over Western Europe— had all but disappeared, thanks partly to the early successes of our policy, partly to the later successes of Soviet science and technology. The world was already a different place, and there were men, like Senator Hennings, who understood this. But instead of challenging the assumptions of our policy, as Hennings had urged, we enlarged them. Just as it was becoming clear that Europe was out of danger, we began to conceive our mission to be a global one and our adversary to be an ideology.

In the first phase of the Cold War—roughly from 1946 to 1950—there had been nothing like the stress on ideology that reached its peak in the early fifties. Although American opinion had always been "anti-Communist," the putative threat in the late forties came not from a dogma but from a particular state, its armies massed on one side of the Iron Curtain, its political agents dispersed on the other. The political character of the regime was well known and held in general disapproval. Though the Truman Doctrine had a globalist ring and now and then American spokesmen talked about the threat of "world Communism," we were not so doctrinaire as to be unable to perceive the advantages of good relations with Communist Yugoslavia when Marshal Tito broke with Marshal Stalin in 1948. The move from a pragmatic to a theological foundation did not come about until after the Communists won China in 1949 and Senator Joe McCarthy won celebrity in 1950. It has often been said that the first of these events had a lot to do with the second—and that the second had a lot to do with the way this country looked at and dealt with the world in the fifties. No doubt there are connections, close ones, but one can at least imagine this change having come about with no assistance from either Mao Tse-tung or Senator McCarthy. What McCarthy knew in his brief career and what Mao Tse-tung has known throughout his long one is that there is among every people on earth a weakness for conspiracy theories of history. Our people are no exception. However, our people may be unique in their yearning for high-sounding moral purpose and political abstraction. Part of our difficulty has always been, as it so manifestly is today, that we cannot be satisfied with limited goals or a morality that is not universally applicable. Opposing an evil doctrine or fighting for a noble one has always been much more appealing to us than expending our energies on so mean-sounding a goal as maintaining or altering the balance of power, a concept our statesmen have always professed to abhor even when it has been central to their thinking.

No sooner was the myth of world Communism exploded than there developed a tendency, in those places where new conspiracy theories are fabricated as replacements for the old, to think that the whole idea was part of a plot to involve us in wars of aggression and domination. The fact is, though, that the original concept of Communism as an international movement, a revolutionary creed and conspiracy seeking mastery of the world, was first put forward not by bourgeois reactionaries but by the Communists themselves. "Workers of the world, unite!" The Communists believed it with at least as much fervor as any anti-Communist ever did, and such events as the defection of Tito and the Sino-Soviet split were far more jarring to them than to those in the West who received the news with some embarrassment, feeling that if they had been thinking straight they would have seen it all coming long before they did. However that may be, there was in the early fifties a certain plausibility in the view that Communist nations could act in concert under some kind of central leadership—and that therefore the conquest of China by Communists increased the formidability of our adversary. Since the Soviet

Union and China were societies with little in common except a long boundary and a professed adherence to the social gospel known as Marxism-Leninism, their ability to coordinate such an assault on Western positions as the war in Korea was impressive, and it did not then seem unreasonable to believe that Communism could foster alliances between nations notably unalike in history and culture.

Had it not been for the upheaval in China and the war in Korea (rather large events to attempt to abstract from history), we might have been able, in the early fifties, to undertake a re-examination of our whole policy. A sensible conclusion might have been that the policy had been a success and that success had made it obsolete. Such a conclusion might have led to the kind of efforts taken later in that decade, after the death of John Foster Dulles, and early in the next one to institutionalize "competitive coexistence" and to remove some of the terror from the balance thereof. But what happened happened, and attention became fixed not on achievement in Europe but on what we convinced ourselves was our failure in Asia. The war in Korea, though it drew little criticism from liberals or intellectuals, was unpopular with the mass of people and counted a symbol of failure. Eisenhower was made President and Dulles was made Secretary of State. Before long,

Dulles was speaking of an "agonizing reappraisal," but what he meant by that was not a painful review of the assumptions of our diplomacy but a reconsideration of our military strategy.

If there was a fatal weakness in George Marshall's concept of buying time for its own sake, it was the failure to take account of the forces of momentum and inertia in politics and diplomacy. Though it may have been clear to everyone involved in its formulation that a particular policy was not intended to function in perpetuity, the policy, once established without a date for termination and without any machinery for review, tended to perpetuate itself. A bureaucracy was established to administer it; when any bureaucracy is compelled to acknowledge that its mission has been completed, in success or in failure, its tendency is to think of new missions that will justify its continued existence. (NATO in recent years has been a fine multinational example of this.) Marshall thought ahead to a time when reasonable men would have a fresh look at the world and, if they felt that circumstances justified it, devise a fresh approach. But no procedure for review was built into the policy;* and since its time-buying as-

* Theoretically, of course, all policies are always under review by the President, the State Department, the appropriate committees of the House and Senate, and public opinion. On short-term policies, these checks often work quite

pect was almost a secret of state, it is hard to see how this might have been accomplished.

Now and then, to be sure, there were signs of uneasiness in high places over the drag of the past on our policies. Eisenhower, Kennedy, and Johnson have all testified to this at one time or another, with Kennedy, in his American University speech of June 10, 1963, almost echoing Marshall as he said that "the tide of time and events will often bring surprising changes in the relations between states" and urged that "we must re-examine our own attitudes— as individuals and as a nation." It was perhaps the most elegant speech of his Presidency, and it contributed greatly to his immediate objective, the Test Ban Treaty that was negotiated that summer and ratified by the Senate in the fall.* Lyndon Johnson

---

effectively; sometimes, too, they prove a hindrance, as in the case of foreign-aid programs which have been rendered less effective than they need be because of congressional insistence on periodic reappraisal. But when a policy is an expression of an ideological commitment—such as anti-Communism—it is as unlikely to be reviewed as a commitment to "democracy" or "free enterprise."

* However, only two weeks later Kennedy was in Berlin and, addressing a vast throng in the Rudolph Wilde Platz, said: "There are many people in the world who really don't understand . . . what is the great issue between the free world and the Communist world. Let them come to Berlin! And there are some who say in Europe and elsewhere we can work with the Communists. Let them come to Berlin!" At that moment his own diplomats were "working with" the Communists on the Test Ban Treaty. It is not easy to escape even the rhetoric of an established policy.

has now and then echoed these sentiments and has driven his subordinates to seek other agreements with the Soviet Union. The fact nevertheless remains that the policy implemented by the war in Vietnam perceives the main threat to our national interest in Communist ideology and in what the President, speaking in San Antonio in September 1967, called "Communist expansionism."

The *New York Times* for January 1, 1968, carried in adjoining columns on its editorial page two commentaries that tell much of how the world we now inhabit differs from that of 1948. One is a column by Robert Kleiman reporting on some quiet negotiations between the Soviet Union and the Federal Republic of Germany. According to Kleiman there was a strong possibility that in the months ahead Moscow and Bonn would compose most of their differences and establish sound relationships. This would come about because, Kleiman wrote: "Moscow's long-term objective is not simply détente, of course, but stabilization of the status quo" in Europe. The "of course" is well placed. Thirteen years at least have passed since Moscow made plain its desire for détente, but it is news—provided it is true—that the Soviet Union has as a "long-term objective" the maintenance of the present balance of power in Europe. Just to the left of the Kleiman column is an editorial entitled "Man vs. Nature." "The turn of the year," the editorialist observes, "is an ideal time to take stock of the damage man is doing to his natural environment." Actually, the turn of the year had nothing to do with it. What made the *Times* sit up and take notice was the previous week's meeting in New York of the American Association for the Advancement of Science at which there had been presented some alarming appraisals of the problems created for humanity by human ingenuity and human fecundity. The editorial went on: "Professor Barry Commoner of Washington University agreed that the environment is being placed under stress 'to the point of collapse' and this planet is approaching 'a crisis which may destroy its suitability as a place for human society.' Professor L. C. Cole of Cornell University suggested that even the continued availability of the earth's oxygen supply can no longer be taken for granted and that the world's population may 'already be beyond what the world can support on a continuing basis.' "

A few days later, the *Times* reported that in the year's first issue of the *Bulletin of the Atomic Scientists*, the Doomsday Clock, a feature of each issue, had been reset. Having for some time been at twelve minutes before midnight, it had now moved

ahead to seven minutes before the hour. The explanation, surprisingly, was not that there were new
tensions between the major nuclear powers and that
new confrontations were likely. What the scientists
feared as the cause of ultimate destruction was the
increase in "violence and nationalism" throughout
the world which could lead to the kind of war the
nuclear powers are currently determined to prevent.

Here, then, is the world we face in 1968. It is a
world not only of the "surprising changes in the
relations between states" which Kennedy foresaw but
of fears and hopes for the future of mankind that
have little or nothing at all to do with conflicts over
power or ideology. If the scientists are to be believed, we can do ourselves in as thoroughly by failing to control the atmosphere as by failing to bring
nuclear weapons under control. In such a world, a
rational diplomacy might regard the balance of nature as being for the present at least as important as
the balance of power. However that may be, and
whatever moral and political judgments may be
made on American policy in Vietnam, what one is
compelled to say is that the war there is, except as
it hinders the practice of a rational diplomacy, mon-
umentally irrelevant to what should be the priorities
of policy in 1968. This is not to say that new circum-

stances require us to be indifferent to the political future of Vietnam and Southeast Asia; a world exposed to new dangers is not less interdependent than formerly. But the problems posed by power do not begin to compare in significance or urgency to the problems of survival—a fact long since acknowledged in practice if not in rhetoric by the original Cold War antagonists. If we can say with any assurance that nationalism transcends ideology, we can say with complete assurance that breathing transcends both, and that neither a Communist victory nor a Communist defeat will purify the atmosphere or avert famine or ease the pressures of population on the total human environment.

To such problems the war in Vietnam is irrelevant except in one crucial sense—that its early conclusion would be the largest single contribution that any nation or group of nations could presently make to the well-being of mankind. For while what is at issue between the contenders in Vietnam can be described as being at most tangential to the great issues in today's world, the war itself—the fact of its existence—delays and makes infinitely more difficult the kind of efforts that are needed to combat the manifold threats to all of us that flow from modern technology and from the political changes that have taken place—and been largely unaffected by the course of the Cold War—in the past two decades. In the first and most practical sense, the costs of the war require this country, richer by far than any other and as a consequence of its technology bearing a heavy responsibility for the new threats to life, to contribute far less than it should to dealing with the new crises. Unable, primarily because of the war, to deal with new sources of tension within our own boundaries, we can devote only the most modest and inadequate share to the international effort which must be made in dealing with the problems that affect the entire globe and all people everywhere. We are neglecting even the kind of research needed merely to anticipate and plan against new hazards of the age which *is* so largely an American creation. For some years, for example, scientists here and abroad have been speaking of the need to control the acquisition of nuclear weapons not only by governments but by private interests, perhaps in time by private persons. The spread of knowledge about the *peaceful* uses of atomic energy and the increasing availability of fissionable materials gives rise to the prospect of nuclear weapons coming into the possession of men who bear no responsibility for the lives and security of anyone except themselves. For a while, the Atomic Energy Commission had a number of scientists exploring this hideous possibility, but in the squeeze caused by the war, most of their research has had to be curtailed.

[ 83 ]

But the cost factor is by no means the only one. Vietnam, itself so irrelevant, deflects our attention from the relevant and is so divisive a force in the world that appropriate international action can rarely be undertaken even when the costs are light. It is plain that no very useful approach can be made to such great problems as hunger, disease, population, and the pollution of the earth's atmosphere unless this country and the European powers, including the Soviet Union, along with Japan and certain other large and industrialized nations can act in some kind of concert. It may well be that without a Western rapprochement with the fourth of humanity living in China, nothing is possible. But it is surely true that the noncooperation between ourselves and the Soviet Union dooms almost every effort toward peace and toward concerted action for any other end. Although we have plenty of evidence that both governments know this and see precisely how damaging noncooperation is to the narrowest national interest of each, Vietnam stands in the way. Neither power has any really vital interest there. Peace would benefit each far more than war does. But a resolution eludes them both. And on this account humanity is more and more in danger of extinction.

# IV

## Thoughts While Trying
## to Face the Music

Though I may here or there in these pages have
used the word "because" lightly or pontifically, I hold
a kind of Tolstoyan view of history, and believe that
it is hardly ever possible to determine the real truth
about how and why we got from here to there. Since
I find it extremely difficult to uncover my own motives, I hesitate to deal with those of other people,
and I positively despair at the thought of ever being
really sure about what has moved whole nations and
whole generations of mankind. No explanation of
the causes and origins of any war—of any large happening in history—can ever be for me much more
than a proximate or plausible one, a reasonable hypothesis. But if, as I see it, we cannot answer the
"how" and "why" questions with anything like certi-

tude, we can answer a good many of the "what" ones, and this sometimes enables us to eliminate at least some of the suggested hows and whys. In regard to Vietnam, I feel confident in isolating certain non-causes and non-origins. Although our role in the Geneva Conference was not, as it turned out, of much help to anyone, it was not the American attitude at the Geneva Conference in 1954 that made what everyone now speaks of as the "Geneva agreements" unworkable. It can easily be argued that they proved unworkable because the Russians gave the French (and the South Vietnamese) better terms than they needed to, in the expectation that the French would on this account decide not to enter the proposed European Defense Community. However that may be, those so-called agreements were not a diplomatic settlement of any kind but simply a statement of the terms of a cease-fire. To quote John McAlister again:

There were only three documents signed at Geneva, and only four signatories were involved: France, the royal governments of Laos and Cambodia, and the Vietminh. [The Vietminh was an army, not a government. What we think of as the South Vietnamese, or anti-Communist Vietnamese, were never consulted.] These agreements were not treaties and they were not formally ratified by any government by any process. They were simply agreements between the opposing military commands to stop the fighting in Indochina and to take measures to prevent the fighting from being resumed. Some confusion has resulted because the "Final Declaration of the Geneva Conference," which "noted" the key provisions of the various cease-fire agreements, seemed to emanate from all nine conference participants. However, this "Final Declaration" was not signed by *any* of the participants. It was yet another Cold War device to mask the lack of consensus among the major powers— an "unsigned treaty."

We have sinned greatly and frequently since 1954, but not always in the ways that we think we have. We did not go into Vietnam in pursuit of an irrelevancy. While it is easy enough for me and for others today to say that we should never have extended the policy of "containment" to Asia and that we should always have known that ideological warfare is absurd, Vietnam in the mid-fifties was not seen as an opportunity for containment or holy war. The rationalizations came, as they almost always do, after the fact. We did not go to Vietnam looking for war or even expecting it; after all, we had just passed up a splendid chance to join the fighting with our then friends the French at our side. We passed it up for a number of reasons—among them a distaste for bloodshed occasioned by our recent experience in Korea (where the fighting had ended only a few months earlier) and the reluctance of our politicians to support a colonial power. True, we were not taken altogether by surprise at discovering that nothing really had been settled by Geneva. Two-fifths of our aid in the early days was military, three-fifths economic, but something beyond this ratio persuades me that we were after something a bit more decent than the opening of a new firing range. The non-Communist state that came into being as a consequence of the Geneva Conference looked to John Foster Dulles and to his foreign-aid people as if it might actually work, as if it might turn out to be a nice, prosperous, well-behaved little democracy. In the bright light of hindsight, this seems a ridiculous dream. We might have known, we can now tell ourselves, that Ngo Dinh Diem and his landholder friends would never let it happen. Perhaps so—in any case, we will never really know. But it would not have been altogether ridiculous to have harbored the suspicion that whatever may have been the intentions of Diem and his associates, Ho Chi Minh would never let it happen. We are always being told what awful people we have supported in Saigon while all along there existed the alternative of supporting the Vietnamese Thomas Jefferson, Ho Chi Minh, and having him working with us—building a friendly Communist society, strengthening Vietnamese nationalism, telling the Chinese to stay where they belong. There are times when Ho sounds a lot more intelligent and interesting than most of the types we have lately been dealing with (since the leaders on both sides seem to have no qualms about murder, that factor more or less cancels out), and it might have been very smart of us back before 1950, say, to try to strike up some sort of deal with him. But Ho could not have been much interested in us in the early fifties (and anyway think of what McCarthy would have said), and Diem then did not have, or was concealing, his cloven hoof. Diem never seemed a Thomas Jefferson, or even a Lyndon Johnson, but he looked no worse than our man in Korea, Syngman Rhee. And one can at least advance the hypothesis that the worst of our troubles have grown not out of Diem's "failure" and ours to create a good society in South Vietnam, but out of a certain amount of early success, or, if not that, out of Ho's fear that we might somehow succeed someday. It could also be that he was not unmindful of the possibilities for looting. The Americans had put a good many desirable things—including a lot of expensive and well-made weaponry—in South Vietnam, and if he could knock over the government without too much difficulty they would all be his.

Senator Fulbright has been saying for years that foreign aid is dangerous because it can lead to war. I

think he is right. We invest money and, more important, hope in a country, and when some thugs
threaten to wreck the country and dash its hopes
and ours we are tempted to police the place. Some of
the most promising governments in Africa, for example, are likely to go to pieces because they are
embroiled in wars that receive less attention than
the one in Vietnam but are nevertheless like it in
being a combination of civil war and of aggression
by aggrieved neighboring states.*

---

* I know from experience how quickly and directly one
can move from thoughts of peace and social progress to
thoughts of military intervention. In the summer of 1966,
I spent some time in Kenya and saw something of the war
being fought against its government and that of Ethiopia
by Somali tribesmen in the northeast and by regular forces
of the Somali Republic. While there were notable differences—mostly in scale and intensity—between that war and
the war in Vietnam, the resemblances were impressive. The
Russians and Chinese were supplying the Somalis, most of
whom were guerrillas. The Somali war aim was the annexation by the Republic of Somali of the territory which was
the theater of war. There was something to be said for the
Somali cause, but nothing at all for the war, which put a
far greater drain on the resources of the countries involved
than the Vietnam war puts on our resources. Feeling very
much in sympathy with the Kenyan effort at nation-building,
I sometimes found myself contemplating the advantages to
all parties of having some kind of "pacification" mission
brought in from the outside. As of this writing, the word
is that the war has been stopped by negotiations sponsored
by the Organization of African Unity. But permanent
peace seems unlikely, and this has been in any case only
one of several similar wars being fought in Africa. They
are overshadowed by the war in Vietnam, and therefore
largely unreported, although some of them may someday
be every bit as great a menace to world peace and stability.

Many of my contemporaries reject as bourgeois and "unhistorical" my view of our present plight and its background. One of them, Alfred Kazin, recently said that we could find the real answer to why we are in Vietnam by acquainting ourselves with the expansionist visions of Washington, Jefferson, and the Adamses. Their dreams of power, he says, were realized by a restless, energetic people who made the best of this continent theirs by 1846. We followed the course of empire westward to the water's edge, and then we went over the water to Hawaii and the Philippines, to Japan and China, meanwhile also striking out not only westward but southward, and northward, and eastward and, later, Moonward and Venusward. In due time, we got to Vietnam. We could no more resist it than we could resist Ohio. It is all to be explained by the way power obeys the laws of power—and more particularly by the way that "great" powers obey the laws of great powerdom. While I think it possible that such laws exist, I have trouble in learning what they are. I cannot find any law or any principle of history that works more often than now and then or explains what I think most in need of explanation.

Obviously there is a connection between our power as a nation and our presence in Vietnam. We are scandalously rich; though we are now feeling the pinch, we still have the money to go on. The French, who now have the nerve to call us aggressors, were not so rich in 1954 and could not afford it. Our being there and doing what we are doing also has much to do with the fact that the French and the British are no longer there. We did our bit in persuading the British to leave India and the Dutch to leave Indonesia, but apart from that we are little to blame for any imbalance of power in Asia, and I do not think, as so many others do, that we are building an "empire" or adding to the one we already have. If they are right, then we are building an empire that hardly anyone wants. When I said this to a friend recently, he asked if I had ever been psychoanalyzed. I said I had missed that part of the rich, full life. A pity, he said, for if I had been, I would know how meaningless it is to say that we don't "want" an empire. The lion doesn't "want" the gazelle; he is simply eating to live. If this is how we got to Vietnam, I would like someone to explain all our unleonine hesitations along the way, the recurrent blindness to our fate among the men who are thought to be the masters of it, and all our present divisions over the present war.

We became a great power in 1918 and annoyed everyone by refusing to act like one. We became a superpower in 1945. Roosevelt, who had so much to do with bringing this to pass, told Churchill it was unthinkable—absolutely out of the question—that there should be American troops in Europe for more than two years after the defeat of Germany. Roosevelt knew us well and was right in saying what he said when he said it. No country ever demobilized so rapidly or so thoroughly as we did after 1945. We gave the stuff away, we threw it away, we put it in mothballs. Even when we joined NATO in 1949, we didn't remobilize; instead we had a hot debate in the Senate as to whether there ought to be any American troops in Europe or anywhere in peacetime. The ayes had it in the end, but it was a close thing. We were hardly more prepared to fight a war in Korea than was Venezuela. We weren't ready for Vietnam either. We had plenty of nuclear warheads, plenty of missiles, and quite a few men under arms, but the Eisenhower administration, which had prepared us only for a war of survival against the Soviet Union, had left us wholly unready for what we were drifting into. John Foster Dulles had signed the contracts, but they were largely a fake; he couldn't have posted a performance bond.

Now I can understand that a nation must obey certain imperatives created for it by its history and its power. It is happening all the time. If history helps in explaining why we are in Vietnam, it also helps in explaining why we seem unable to get out. But I cannot understand why a nation that, according to the "determinists," has been heading in the same direction for fifty or a hundred or, as Alfred Kazin would have it, almost two hundred years always seems so uncertain of what to do next. Not all our leaders have been fools. Though I am unable to see it, this nation may have an irresistible subconscious yen to dominate the world, but news of it should by now have reached the conscious minds of some of our leaders, who should at least be awake and ready when the moment of fulfillment is at hand. Awake and ready they have seldom been. And today, when we are at the height of our power, the news that is reaching them is that a great part of the country damned well doesn't want to fulfill its destiny if this means having their sons lose their lives at Khesanh or lose their humanity in some travesty of a school in the ghetto.

In our past, as in our present, there was much that was ugly about our means of expansion and our policy toward others. We made ourselves a continental nation by swindles, by violence, by trickery—but more by the hard and lonesome work of people who were not crooks or hoodlums or con men. Of course we could not resist going into Ohio and all the way on to the Pacific and then, as traders and at times as soldiers, on to Asia. But we did not always go as conquerors. Our westward movement, in which the war with Mexico was only incidental, involved little conquest, and was no more "imperialist" than the settlement of  Massachusetts. Those whom Henry Thoreau thought we were mistreating had seized the land with violence and had not only massacred Indians but held them in large numbers as slaves. More important, while Mexico had as good a claim as anyone else to the land, it was either not governing it at all—because the governors couldn't enforce their writ across such distances—or misgoverning. Much of the Southwest was occupied without anyone firing a shot, and Spaniards in Santa Fe (who thought of themselves as Spaniards conquered by Mexicans twenty-five years earlier) welcomed General S. W. Kearny's Army of the West as an army of liberation. If ever there was a case of power filling up a vacuum which nature abhors, it was the war Thoreau abhorred.

In a recently published symposium called *Authors Take Sides on Vietnam*, the American playwright Paddy Chayevsky writes: "I think we are in Vietnam to set up a large force in Southeast Asia in preparation for a war with China." The note is struck by many others and is a favorite with the American Empire school. But if a war with China is what we want, why in 1968 are we fighting—with so little success, with such heavy losses—in so unsuitable a place as South Vietnam. If this is a warmup, it is the stupidest one in history. If a war against China has been regarded as necessary or inevitable for many years, we could have mounted it a lot sooner and under far more favorable conditions. We have better bases than Vietnam in Korea and Formosa. In a study of our postwar Asian policy published in the *Vassar Alumni News*, Carl Degler shows that our approach to Communist China has been consistent only in the sense that it has been consistently vacillating and uncertain. In 1947, two years before the issue was finally joined, we abandoned our effort to form a Nationalist-Communist coalition government. "After that," Degler writes, "the United States ceased to intervene in the Chinese civil war." By 1949, the Communists were in power on the mainland and Chiang Kai-shek had withdrawn to Formosa. Our policy, as Dean Acheson put it, was to wait "for the dust to settle." In a famous speech before the National Press Club in January 1950, Acheson placed not only Korea but Chiang's Formosa outside our "defense perimeter." The assault on South Korea led the government to change its mind. It did so, according to Degler, not to use Formosa as a staging area or even to guarantee its permanent security, but because "it believed that if Formosa should fall into the hands of the Chinese Communists, the American position in Korea would be outflanked and endangered." But though the containment of China was one of our major aims then, as it remains today, we did not take General MacArthur's advice and carry the war beyond the Yalu. And when there was a truce in Korea, even though many friends of Chiang were powerful in the new administration, we did not provoke China or "unleash," to use a favorite verb of the period, the Generalissimo. We subsidized the French in Indochina, but declined to move in and build bases there.

In the mid-fifties and on into the early sixties, there were many members of this government with no appetite for war with China or anyone else who felt that we should give Saigon substantial economic aid and enough military assistance to stand on its own feet and have the time and energy to make something of the country. They were motivated to a large degree by an anti-Communism that they should have recognized as an unsound and unworthy basis for policy, and it is now clear to everyone that they were blind to the realities of Vietnamese life. However, what they were attempting to do in Vietnam was not very different from what they were attempting to do in a good many other underdeveloped countries—and at times being rewarded with a certain amount of success. Though anti-Communism has led us to support some manifestly insupportable regimes (antifascism had earlier done the same thing), it has also led us to give well-used aid—military as well as economic—to governments making a determined struggle to build decent and humane societies. It is true that we counseled against the holding of Vietnamese national elections in 1956, and it may be true that had we let well enough alone, the two Vietnams might have become one with relatively little bloodshed. (It is hard to believe, in the light of all that has subsequently happened, that with or without American intervention, the unification would have come about as a result of the kind of free and open elections envisaged by those critics who claim that the Eisenhower administration sabotaged democracy in Vietnam. There was no attachment to democracy among the leaders of any faction in Vietnam, North or South.) At any rate, there was at the time no large-scale violence in Vietnam, and although violence might have been foreseen, there was little reason to think that any difficulties with the Vietcong would have much to do with the balance of power beyond the borders of Vietnam itself. Indeed—and here, perhaps, is another important difference between this war and the war in Korea—it seems to have been *our* military presence, and not that of the Communists, that gave the war a real balance-of-power meaning.

When Kennedy took office, Vietnam was not our main concern even on the peninsula once known as Indochina. Laos was a far more troublesome place then, and there was general agreement in the new administration that in Laos there was no hope for a military solution. In time, largely because the Russians were looking the other way, a political settlement of sorts was made, and, unsatisfactory though it was, there were few objections to it here or abroad. In that period, the "domino theory"—that the fall of any given state would lead to the fall of its nearest neighbor and so on almost *ad infinitum*—was generally discredited. There may then have been a chance for a President to have reappraised our commitment to Saigon and to have ordered a phase-out. Vietnam was still an obscure place, and with us no longer involved, it would have become still more obscure. Kennedy could probably have de-escalated, but instead he escalated. Had he lived, and had he beaten Goldwater or some other Republican in 1964, he might have altered his strategy at some later point—perhaps when it became clear, as it did in mid-1965, that the only hope for the regime in Saigon was a thorough Americanization of the war. But he died, and Johnson went on escalating. If we had got out of Vietnam five years ago, the balance of power in Asia might have been affected only insignificantly and imperceptibly. If we got out tomorrow, the consequences—at least in Asia—would be large and from almost any point of view undesirable.

I believe this to be so because, unlike many others who favor disengagement, I do not today believe that the domino theory is quite the joke it is so widely held to be. It has, to be sure, no demonstrable merit or validity as a principle of history. While the world grows in interdependence and the devaluation of sterling necessarily is felt in our economy, it is on the face of it absurd to say that if South Vietnam falls, so in time will the Philippines, and in due course Australia and perhaps even Mexico will follow suit. But if, as a proposition of that sort, it is nonsense, it has at the same time a peculiar validity that is anything but innate but that has been lent it by the way John Foster Dulles conducted American foreign policy during his stewardship and by the way it has been conducted over the last few years. When Dulles set up the Southeast Asia Treaty Organization—and negotiated similar treaties, bilateral and multilateral, elsewhere in the world—he connected, by the steel thread of American military aid, states that had few, if any, other connections with one another. All of these governments have been encouraged to rely on us for their defense, and most of them, of course, have been only too happy to do so. Thus, if any part of this unfortunate network collapsed because we declined to defend it with American lives, the effect elsewhere would probably be enormous. Had these governments not been led to place so much reliance on us, this would not be the case. But as things have worked out, some dominos might fall in a certain way because we set them up that way.

We are in Vietnam, Dean Rusk has said, "because we made a promise. We have made promises in other parts of the world. If Moscow or Peking ever discovers that the promises of the United States do not mean what they say, then this world goes up in smoke." Here is administration rhetoric at its most alarmist and disingenuous—yet it is not wholly to be disregarded. We have made promises we had no business making and, as Moscow and Peking long ago "discovered," are incompetent to fulfill. Nevertheless, several small nations took us at our word and planned their own policies accordingly, so that there can be today little doubt that American disengagement in Vietnam, though it might be the most beneficial thing we could do for the world at large and for our own disintegrating society, would be disastrous or almost so to those Southeast Asian countries that signed up for the American insurance policies that Dulles was peddling in the mid-fifties. It is not unlikely that several of them would face insurrections—"wars of national liberation"—and invasion on the model of Vietnam and without hope of outside assistance.*

Until early in 1965, I felt that our role in Vietnam was, though unwise, defensible. The rulers of the country seemed an untrustworthy lot, but that did not appear a sufficient reason for turning the place over to the Vietcong. Convinced that a poor nation cannot manage war and development at the same time without assistance, I felt that our assistance in putting down an insurgency was helpful. The fact

---

* Save possibly from the Soviet Union. A Soviet version of the domino theory has lately been set forth in the *Literaturnaya Gazeta* of Moscow. Under the name of Ernst Henri, the Marxist commentator Semyon Rostovsky has written that China has a three-stage military plan for including in its " 'Reich,' apart from China itself, Korea, the Mongolian People's Republic, Vietnam, Cambodia, Laos, Indonesia, Malaysia, Burma, and several other countries in that region." Rostovsky quotes some items of Maoist propaganda but is not very specific about how the schedule could be kept. However, he is alarmed enough to call the plan "a historical crime against the international working-class movement," and it is clear that he thinks the main thrust of Soviet policy today should be the prevention of Chinese hegemony in the states he names.

that the insurgents were natives did not bother me;
so were their antagonists, and I have never believed
that civil wars are somehow more virtuous and rational than wars of any other kind. They are, as a
rule, the very bloodiest sort. From my point of view,
the operations of the Vietcong were, and still are,
every bit as irrational as I now believe ours are.
They don't seem to mind destroying their country
any more than we do. I can understand why some
Americans should be indifferent to the fate of Vietnam—to a certain degree, and to my own dismay, I
am coming to feel that way myself—but I cannot
understand why any Vietnamese should be indifferent to it. I wish Johnson would swallow his pride,
whatever the consequences, but it seems to me it is
positively idiotic for Ho Chi Minh not to take Johnson and Rusk at their word and, if what they are
saying is all a bluff, call it. Why not set a place and
a date, and see whether Rusk shows up? Everybody
knows that unless American forces stay in Vietnam
for the rest of history the Vietcong are going to have
their triumphs anyway; if they negotiated us out of
there tomorrow on any terms at all, the country
would be theirs before long. If the Vietcong can re-
main as strong as they seem to be with all the Americans chasing them around the country, they should
have no trouble at all seizing power after they sat

down and told us enough lies about the future to make it impossible for us not to agree to get out. The American people love to be lied to at peace conferences, and if that happened in this instance the guerrilla could put away his shooting irons, turn respectable, run for office, and run the country. General Ky could get a job with Pan American World Airways or just loll about on the Riviera, where he would be an authentic part of the scene and would find a lot of his old friends as well as many new ones.

No such denouement is in prospect. The Westernized, Frenchified Saigon generals might find happiness on the beach at Cannes, but Ho Chi Minh is an Asian revolutionary, a nation-builder whose aim today is the humiliation of the United States. He does not look upon his revolution as one imagines a European Marxist-Leninist would in similar circumstances. Surely a Lenin or a Tito, seeing so many roads to eventual political victory, would not insist upon taking the longest and costliest one. Ho and his comrades cannot be indifferent to the fate of their country, but they can be—they obviously are— indifferent to the bricks and mortar that have been pulverized by our bombs and to the life and death of peasants who themselves seem so indifferent and resigned to fate. By the military calculus of the

Pentagon, they cannot possibly win the war as long as we are engaged—ergo, they will in time be compelled to settle on terms acceptable to us. But as they must see it, they have already won many famous victories. They have shown how the greatest military power in history can be defied for years on end by a vastly inferior force. Their guerrillas have tied down more than forty percent of our combat-ready divisions, more than fifty percent of our air power, more than a third of our naval strength. Their war has done more to divide us from one another and our country from others than anything the Soviet Union or China has ever managed. A day may come when they will feel that their point has been made and that it is time to think about the cadres they are losing and about the agonies that they—along with us—are inflicting on the Vietnamese people. But we cannot count on it. We have as yet given them no reason to doubt that they are marching in step with history and toward a high destiny.

For Ho's generals, given their view of the war and its role in nation-building, the outlook may seem anything but discouraging. In North Vietnam alone, about two hundred thousand young men reach military age each year. Thus far, if we accept as reasonably accurate the figures our government asks us to accept, the most we have been able to do is to remove from combat—by killing, by wounding, by capturing—something less than half that number. This, of course, includes guerrillas recruited in the South—and it almost certainly includes some non-combatants. But even if the figures were double what the Pentagon claims, and even if we faced no adversaries except the North Vietnamese regulars, Hanoi would have each year a surplus of at least one hundred thousand—and an accumulated surplus many times that large. This is the basic arithmetic of the war, and with such a margin, and with a belief that the glory lies in the battle itself, why should they wish to negotiate?

If there is to be peace, we will have to make it, and we may have to think more in terms of withdrawal (a euphemism, it cannot be denied, for defeat) than in terms of negotiations. Although it will do no harm to keep announcing that it is a negotiated settlement we seek, we should make peace rather than negotiation our primary aim, and we should not delude ourselves into thinking that anything desirable—such as an end to the carnage— would necessarily come of negotiations. Indeed, a conference that failed to produce an armistice within a matter of weeks might only heighten the danger. Negotiations unaccompanied by a measurable de-escalation would only add to the desperation on our side and thus to the likelihood of nuclear war. If it became apparent, as it almost certainly would, that what our Secretary of State calls "the other side" was filibustering—that it had no intention of telling us the sweet lies that would enable us to believe that we were buying peace with "honor"—Washington would find it increasingly difficult to resist the clamor to use all the power we have. Until recently, I felt that the best first move would be a relatively small one—small but conspicuous: not necessarily an end to all bombing but the announcement and execution of a plan for scaling it down to the point at which it could be justified only in terms of the security of our forces. This, I felt, might soon be followed by a suspension of all search-and-destroy missions by American troops and the adoption of some version of the "enclaves" strategy recommended two years ago by General James M. Gavin. I did not think that such moves would be of the least help in "bringing Hanoi to the conference table," but I thought they might put an end to our scaring everyone else about our intentions, particularly toward the Chinese, and would help in preparing us for the inevitable. But now it may be too late for any kind of phased withdrawal. In early 1968, the nature of the war changed radically. The Vietcong brought it to the cities, and the North Vietnamese carried it to the most strongly fortified of our installations. The biggest search-and-destroy missions of the war were mounted against us, and the enclaves themselves were threatened. The contention that while we might never be able to win a military victory we could not possibly suffer a military defeat became rather a shaky one.

We may be facing, then, a choice between disastrous escalation and a large- or even full-scale unilateral de-escalation that no amount of press-agentry could redeem with talk of new "priorities" or "schedules" or "targets." Walter Lippmann has gone so far as to advocate a withdrawal to Australia. It would be preferable to escalation or even to the continuation of the war as it was being fought in late 1967. But I do not see how the Johnson administration could undertake any sort of de-escalation without some form of collaboration from North Vietnam and the National Liberation Front. Theodore C. Sorensen writes that since Khrushchev could admit a mistake in the missile crisis five years ago, and Kennedy could acknowledge one at the Bay of Pigs a year before that, Lyndon Johnson ought to be able to do the same thing now. Here are two analogies that do not work at all. The missile crisis was over in a few days, the Bay of Pigs crisis in a few hours. No Russian soldiers died in the missile crisis, no American ones at the Bay of Pigs. It would take greater magnanimity and a greater dedication to the truth than we have any right to expect of any politician on earth for Lyndon Johnson to say that this whole bloody business is a mistake, and was from the start.

The administration has painted itself in. For that reason, I can conceive of voting for a Republican candidate in the hope that another President, almost any other President, could disengage, as Eisenhower did in Korea in 1953, without personal humiliation. But for me it is a frail hope. For one thing, there is no Eisenhower seeking the Presidency today. For another, there is no evidence that our adversaries have any intention of letting us off the hook. Johnson does not control the options now, and neither he nor any successor is likely to control them next year. I doubt that in our present situation we could change the policies by changing the men. But it is about the only option we have.

Whether there is peace or continued war in Vietnam, we are in for a siege of ugly political strife here—not only in the 1968 election but in the years that will follow, no matter who wins in November. It will be ugly no matter what happens in Vietnam. When any nation fails in a great and costly undertaking, it conducts a search for those on whom the failure may be blamed. Though it was never within our power to prevent the fall of Chiang Kai-shek's China, that event precipitated a hunt for American scapegoats that went on for five years. Few American lives were lost in or as a consequence of the Chinese civil war. As I write, more than sixteen thousand gallant Americans have met death in Vietnam. A government that lost the war there or withdrew from it without having achieved any of its declared aims would be a government that had sent men to die in vain, in a hopeless, inglorious cause. Not only the political opposition but the country as a whole would demand an accounting.

The guilty would soon enough be found: Lyndon Johnson, Hubert Humphrey, Dean Rusk, Robert McNamara—and on down to the lowest echelons of aides and advisers. Those who oppose the war may say that this group has richly earned the obloquy that would descend upon it. Perhaps so, but it would hardly end there. The doves would fall alongside the hawks—and in greater number. For nothing is easier or more plausible than to blame defeat on those who stirred dissension and counseled retreat. Indeed, we already see the administration trying to save itself by attacking the critics. And there is a case of sorts: though dissent may often be the only honorable course a man can take, there can be no doubt that when it becomes widespread it weakens the nation's will to follow the course to which it has, ignobly or otherwise, committed itself. In any event, the roster of the guilty would include William Fulbright and Robert Kennedy along with the Secretary of State, and Wayne Morse and Eugene McCarthy along with the Secretary of Defense.

There would, in short, be a great purge. In the upper reaches of government, it might be conducted with a certain amount of propriety—no bloodletting, no imprisonment, but rather through free elections, congressional investigations, and other forms of due process. The younger and less prominent dissenters—those who had resisted the draft and those who had abetted them—would probably face graver tribulations. I think it is all in the making and that it may be far worse than the McCarthy years. And the worst of it would probably be that it would undercut the hopes of those who wish to see this war ended because they wish to see this nation deal humanely and vigorously with the inequalities and hatreds that are presently tearing it apart, as well as with those worldwide problems of survival to which the war is so demonstrably irrelevant. As most opponents of the war profess to see it, getting out of Vietnam will liberate us and enable us to take up where we left off in 1965 with the war on poverty, with the reconstruction of our cities, with aid to the developing nations. I wish I could share this hope, but I cannot. It seems to me far more likely that the war on poverty would end with the war in Vietnam, if indeed it is not ended already. For it happens that both wars have had the same sponsorship, the same management, the same political support. The demagogues who would surely arise to exploit the failure in Vietnam would seek to discredit the administration's domestic policies along with its foreign policies. And they would be more eager to remove from public life those who supported the domestic programs than those who supported the foreign programs.

I may be wrong in this appraisal. We are not a reactionary people, and our political instincts are for the most part decent ones. We have a long-standing commitment to our own version of the welfare state, never more powerfully asserted than in the election of 1964. But Johnson's 1964 consensus has been shattered—not only by the war but by the tensions in the cities. If we survive as a nation, it will someday be reconstituted. But the present Congress is well to the right of the one it succeeded, and unless there is a dramatic turn—unimaginable to me at the present time—in the President's fortunes, the next Congress will be more conservative than this one. If the war were over, it would be likely either to return the thirty billion dollars a year now being spent on the war to the taxpayers or to spend them to turn this country into a fortress. I would give odds on the latter.

We deceive ourselves cruelly if we suppose that an end to the war will in itself bring an end to our sufferings here. And we deceive ourselves too if we think that all the consequences overseas would be to the good. I have repeatedly been given pause by the fact that our leading authorities on Asia, men who for the most part bear no responsibility for our present policies and are out of sympathy with some of them, have hesitated to condemn our intervention as flatly as I am inclined to do. Two years ago, Senator Fulbright summoned some of them—including John King Fairbank of Harvard and Doak Barnett of Columbia—before the Senate Foreign Relations Committee and was taken by surprise when their testimony was not altogether unfavorable to administration policy. In general they held the view of one of the most eminent among them, Edwin O. Reischauer, who in 1967 argued, in *Beyond Vietnam: The United States and Asia,* that of the three options he felt were then available—escalation and a probable war with China, complete withdrawal as soon as possible, and plodding along on our present bloody and repugnant course—the last was the least disastrous and hence the most acceptable. Reischauer is a humanist who has great affection for the people of Asia, among whom he lived and studied for many years before John F. Kennedy appointed him ambassador to Japan in 1961. He is no hawk, no imperialist, no warrior of any kind. He thinks we were mistaken ever to become involved in this war and mistaken not to have repaired the error some years back. He holds no brief for the war. But what he fears is that if we leave now we will tell ourselves that Asia and its people are hopeless and that we will abandon the whole continent, with the likely exception of Japan. We might look upon Asia as we looked upon Europe after 1918. To some, this would hardly be a regrettable development. If we can do no better than we have in Vietnam, we would serve the Asians as well as ourselves by leaving the continent alone. But, as Reischauer points out, our policy in Asia has had its successes as well as its failures. If we have destroyed Asian lives, we have also saved them. It would make little sense to stop the saving along with the killing. Yet exactly that might be in prospect if we withdrew to Australia, among our own kind of people, and solaced ourselves with the thought that

Asia, even with our help, can never solve its problems. I want to go on having an American presence in Asia because I don't want people to starve if we can prevent it and because I don't want Asians to despise my children and grandchildren.

Nor, many Asian scholars maintain, would it be helpful to withdraw militarily from Asia. Not all the dangers to the peace there come from Vietnam or from our intervention. There are tensions not of our making between China and the Soviet Union, between China and India, between India and Pakistan, and an American withdrawal would at the very least lead some non-nuclear Asian powers to reconsider the advantages of acquiring nuclear weapons. For a time, such considerations put me in substantial agreement with Reischauer and some of his fellow Asianists. But now we seem to be reaching a point at which the argument no longer holds water. For one thing, if we continue much longer we will pull out of the rest of Asia whether we win, lose, or draw in Vietnam. It happens to be the view of our people that they don't want their sons killed so that Asians can go on eating. Most of them would see no logic in saying there is a necessary connection between starvation in India and Americans getting shot in Vietnam, but even if the logic were self-evident they would reject it. And beyond all that, we seem as incapable as the South Vietnamese of running a war—or, at any rate, *this* war—and doing anything worthwhile at the same time. Congress insists on cutting our decent programs elsewhere in the world—to say nothing of those in this country—almost to the point of absurdity. In a literal sense, it is finding a way to make the wretched of the earth foot the bill for Vietnam. This isn't its intention, and as a nation we are still more generous than most, yet not only are innocent people dying in Vietnam but, because of the dollars-and-cents cost of the war, they are dying in many other parts of the world.

These are the worst of American times. We are in a war that threatens all mankind, that can liberate no one, that is irrelevant to our proper concerns as a nation among nations, that acts as an acid on the ties that bind us as a people. Ending it would solve few of the problems it has done so much to exacerbate. But going on with it becomes daily more unconscionable. Our leaders cannot bring it to an end—not because they do not know how, but because they fear, and rightly, that they cannot at once govern and acknowledge folly. They will be compelled to end it only when those they lead reach them with the message that neither can they govern while perpetuating folly.